Lecture Notes in Computer Science 16160

The series Lecture Notes in Computer Science (LNCS), including its subseries Lecture Notes in Artificial Intelligence (LNAI) and Lecture Notes in Bioinformatics (LNBI), has established itself as a medium for the publication of new developments in computer science and information technology research, teaching, and education.

LNCS enjoys close cooperation with the computer science R & D community, the series counts many renowned academics among its volume editors and paper authors, and collaborates with prestigious societies. Its mission is to serve this international community by providing an invaluable service, mainly focused on the publication of conference and workshop proceedings and postproceedings. LNCS commenced publication in 1973.

Min Luo · Liang-Jie Zhang
Editors

Services Computing – SCC 2025

22nd International Conference
Held as Part of the Services Conference Federation, SCF 2025
Hong Kong, China, September 27–30, 2025
Proceedings

Springer

Editors
Min Luo
Georgia Tech
Atlanta, GA, USA

Liang-Jie Zhang
Shenzhen University
Shenzhen, China

ISSN 0302-9743 ISSN 1611-3349 (electronic)
Lecture Notes in Computer Science
ISBN 978-3-032-06319-9 ISBN 978-3-032-06320-5 (eBook)
https://doi.org/10.1007/978-3-032-06320-5

This Springer imprint is published by the registered company Springer Nature Switzerland AG
The registered company address is: Gewerbestrasse 11, 6330 Cham, Switzerland

Preface

Services account for a major part of the IT industry today. Companies increasingly like to focus on their core expertise area and use IT services to address all their peripheral needs. Services computing is a new science that aims to study and better understand the foundations of this highly popular industry. It covers the science and technology of leveraging computing and information technology to model, create, operate, and manage business services.

The 2025 International Conference on Services Computing (SCC 2025) contributed to building the pillars of this important science and shaping the future of services computing. The event was a prime international forum for both researchers and industry practitioners to exchange the latest fundamental advances in the state of the art and practice of business modeling, business consulting, solution creation, service delivery, and software architecture design, development, and deployment.

This volume presents the papers accepted at SCC 2025, held in Hong Kong, China during September 27–30, 2025. SCC 2025 accepted 7 full papers from 11 submissions. Each was reviewed and selected by at least three independent members of the Program Committee in a single-blind review process.

We are pleased to thank the authors whose submissions and participation made this conference possible. We also want to express our thanks to the Organizing Committee and Program Committee members, for their dedication in helping to organize the conference and reviewing the submissions. We owe special thanks to the on-site speakers for their impressive speeches.

September 2025

Min Luo
Liang-Jie Zhang

Organization

Program Chair

Min Luo — Georgia Tech, USA

Services Conference Federation (SCF 2025)

General Chairs

Ali Arsanjani — Google, USA
Wu Chou — Essenlix Corporation, USA

Program Chair

Liang-Jie Zhang — Shenzhen University, China

CFO

Min Luo — Georgia Tech, USA

Operation Committee

Jing Zeng — China Gridcom Co., Ltd., China
Yishuang Ning — Tsinghua University, China
Sheng He — Kingdee International Software Group Co., Ltd., China
Zhuolin Mei — Jiujiang University, China

Steering Committee

Calton Pu (Co-chair) — Georgia Tech, USA
Liang-Jie Zhang (Co-chair) — Shenzhen University, China

SCC 2025 Program Committee

Shigeru Hosono	Tokyo University of Technology, Japan
Muhammad Younas	Oxford Brookes University, UK
Sanjay R. Chaudhary	Ahmedabad University, India
Andre Luis Schwerz	Federal University of Technology - Paraná, Brazil
Jun Shen	University of Wollongong, Australia

Conference Sponsor – Services Society

The Services Society (S2) is a non-profit professional organization that has been created to promote worldwide research and technical collaboration in services innovations among academia and industrial professionals. Its members are volunteers from industry and academia with common interests. S2 is registered in the USA as a "501(c) organization", which means that it is an American tax-exempt nonprofit organization. S2 collaborates with other professional organizations to sponsor or co-sponsor conferences and to promote an effective services curriculum in colleges and universities. S2 initiates and promotes a "Services University" program worldwide to bridge the gap between industrial needs and university instruction.

The Services Sector accounted for 79.5% of the GDP of the USA in 2016. The Services Society has formed 5 Special Interest Groups (SIGs) to support technology- and domain-specific professional activities.

- Special Interest Group on Services Computing (SIG-SC)
- Special Interest Group on Big Data (SIG-BD)
- Special Interest Group on Cloud Computing (SIG-CLOUD)
- Special Interest Group on Artificial Intelligence (SIG-AI)
- Special Interest Group on Metaverse (SIG-Metaverse)

About the Services Conference Federation (SCF)

As the founding member of the Services Conference Federation (SCF), the first **International Conference on Web Services (ICWS)** was held in June 2003 in Las Vegas, USA. Meanwhile, the First International Conference on Web Services - Europe 2003 (ICWS-Europe 2003) was held in Germany in October 2003. ICWS-Europe 2003 was an extended event of the 2003 International Conference on Web Services (ICWS 2003) in Europe. In 2004, ICWS-Europe was changed to the European Conference on Web Services (ECOWS), which was held in Erfurt, Germany.

Sponsored by the Services Society and Springer, SCF 2018 and SCF 2019 were held successfully on June 25 – June 30, 2018, in Seattle, USA, and on June 25 – June 30, 2019, in San Diego, USA. SCF 2020 and SCF 2021 were held successfully online and in satellite sessions in Shenzhen, China. SCF 2022 and 2023 were held successfully on December 10–14, 2022 and on September 23–26, 2023, in Hawaii, USA. SCF 2024 was held successfully on November 16–19, 2024, in Bangkok, Thailand. To celebrate its 23rd birthday, SCF 2025 was held on September 27–30, 2025, in Hong Kong, China.

In the past 22 years, the ICWS community has expanded from Web engineering innovations to scientific research for the whole services industry. Service delivery platforms have been expanded to mobile platforms, the Internet of Things, cloud computing, and edge computing. The services ecosystem has gradually been enabled, value-added, and intelligence embedded through enabling technologies such as big data, artificial intelligence, and cognitive computing. In the coming years, all transactions with multiple parties involved will be transformed into blockchain and metaverse.

Based on technology trends and best practices in the field, the Services Conference Federation (SCF) will continue serving as the conference umbrella's code name for all services-related conferences. SCF 2025 defined the future of New ABCDE (AI, Blockchain, Cloud, BigData, & IOT) and entered the 5G for Services Era. **The theme of SCF 2025 was Services Agent.** We are very proud to announce that SCF 2025's 10 co-located theme topic conferences all centered around "services", with each focusing on exploring different themes (web-based services, cloud-based services, Big Data-based services, services innovation lifecycle, AI-driven ubiquitous services, blockchain-driven trust service ecosystems, industry-specific services and applications, and emerging service-oriented technologies).

- **Bigger Platform:** The 10 collocated conferences (SCF 2025) were sponsored by the Services Society, which is the world-leading not-for-profit organization (501(c)(3)) dedicated to the service of more than 30,000 worldwide Services Computing researchers and practitioners. A bigger platform means bigger opportunities for all volunteers, authors, and participants. Meanwhile, Springer provided sponsorship of the best paper awards and other professional activities. All the 10 conference proceedings of SCF 2025 were published by Springer and indexed in the ISI Conference

Proceedings Citation Index (included in Web of Science), Engineering Index EI (Compendex and Inspec databases), DBLP, Google Scholar, IO-Port, MathSciNet, Scopus, and ZBlMath.

- **Brighter Future:** While celebrating the 2025 version of ICWS, SCF 2025 highlighted the International Conference on AI and Multimodal Services (AIMS 2025) to build the fundamental infrastructure for enabling AIGC services ecosystems. It will also lead our community members to create their own brighter future.
- **Better Model:** SCF 2025 continued to leverage the invented Conference Blockchain Model (CBM) to innovate the organizing practices for all the 10 theme conferences. Senior researchers in the field are welcome to submit proposals to serve as CBM Ambassador for an individual conference to start better interactions during your leadership role in organizing future SCF conferences.

We look forward to your great contributions as a volunteer, author, and conference participant for the fast-growing worldwide services innovations community. If you would like to contribute to SCF 2026 as a leading volunteer or try the new Conference Blockchain Model, please feel free to contact us to become a conference volunteer. For other queries or questions, please feel free to visit our conference websites and find contact information on SCF 2026.

All the invited talks and paper presentations of SCF 2020, SCF 2021, and SCF 2022 are open to all Services Society community members for free. You can watch all presentations through SCF 365.

Contents

Contents

Intelligent Technology and New–Quality Productivity: Shenzhen's Digital Leapfrog

Kunjing Zhang(✉)

Shenzhen Institute of Information Technology, Guangdong 518172, China
2013100916@sziit.edu.cn

Abstract. This study examines how Shenzhen, China's pioneering special economic zone, leverages intelligent technologies to drive new-quality productivity (NQP) through a distinctive digital leapfrog model. The research employs a mixed-methods approach combining panel data analysis of 1,200 enterprises (2018–2025), spatial econometric modeling, and qualitative case studies to investigate three core questions: how institutional innovation enables technological leapfrogging, what governance mechanisms resolve the centralization-vulnerability paradox, and how technology-society co-evolution generates sustainable productivity gains.

Empirical findings reveal that Shenzhen achieves NQP advancement through three interconnected mechanisms: enterprise-level capability restructuring (82.7% probability of TFP growth), industrial integration (0.83% productivity increase per 1% AI penetration), and adaptive urban governance (57% higher public data utilization). The study identifies four replicable leapfrog patterns: technology-skipping in traditional sectors, modular globalization of production, governance fitness through regulatory sandboxes, and resilience reshaping via dual-loop learning. These patterns collectively demonstrate how strategic integration of artificial intelligence, blockchain, and IoT systems—when coupled with institutional innovation—enables regions to bypass incremental development stages, achieving 47% efficiency gains in AI training and 29.4% GDP growth in digital-industrial clusters.

Theoretically, this research re-conceptualizes NQP as a socio-technical achievement emerging from recursive technology-institution interactions, challenging path dependency theories. Practically, it provides policymakers with evidence-based frameworks for accelerating digital transformation while balancing innovation, regulation, and ethical compliance.

Keywords: New-Quality Productivity · Digital Leapfrogging · Intelligent Technology · Institutional Innovation · Shenzhen Model · Productivity Transformation

1 Introduction

The emergence of new-quality productivity (NQP) represents a fundamental shift from traditional productivity paradigms, characterized by its core attributes of high technology, high efficiency, and high quality. As advanced economies increasingly rely on intelligent technologies to drive growth, China's Shenzhen has pioneered a distinctive digital

M. Luo and L.-J. Zhang (Eds.): SCC 2025, LNCS 16160, pp. 1–12, 2026.
https://doi.org/10.1007/978-3-032-06320-5_1

leapfrog model that bypasses incremental technological evolution through strategic integration of artificial intelligence, blockchain, and IoT systems. This model demonstrates a 47% increase in AI training efficiency and 29.4% GDP growth in digital-industrial clusters, significantly outperforming conventional development pathways [1].

Shenzhen's approach provides a critical counterpoint to prevailing innovation theories that emphasize path dependency [15]. By leveraging institutional adaptability and technological modularity, the city has achieved what we term "institutional leapfrogging"—where governance innovations precede and enable technological deployment. This phenomenon challenges the linear technology adoption curves (Rogers, 2003) and offers a replicable framework for latecomer regions seeking accelerated digital transformation [1, 2].

This study investigates three unresolved questions in NQP theory:

(1) How do latecomer advantages enable regions to bypass technological lock-in through institutional innovation?
(2) What governance mechanisms resolve the centralization-vulnerability paradox in data-driven productivity systems?
(3) How does the technology-society co-evolution generate sustainable productivity leapfrogging?

2 Literature Review

2.1 NQP Theory

NQP represents an advanced productive force fundamentally reconfigured by scientific and technological innovation, characterized by disruptive technological breakthroughs and sustainable development paradigms.

Unlike traditional productivity forms, NQP emerges from revolutionary technological breakthroughs, innovative factor allocation, and deep industrial upgrading. Chen and Li (2019) identified its operational mechanisms through three value chain segments: intelligent R&D → smart manufacturing → digital marketing, forming a closed-loop innovation ecosystem [3] (Table 1).

Table 1. Shenzhen's implementation framework demonstrates a multi-level advancement model:

Level	Mechanism	Shenzhen Evidence
Micro (Enterprise)	Disruptive technology adoption	Pengcheng Yunnao III supercomputing infrastructure achieving 47% AI training efficiency improvement [4]
Meso (Industry)	Digital-real economy integration	Longhua District's industrial clusters showing 29.4% GDP growth through digitalization [5]
Macro (Society)	Urban governance restructuring	"Future City Scenario Lab" deploying 8 digital governance scenarios [6]

This tripartite This tripartite model reveals that NQP advancement requires simultaneous progression in technological capability, institutional innovation, and ethical governance [7, 8].

2.2 Intelligent Technology Mechanisms

(1) **Embodied Intelligence and Human-Like Control**
Recent breakthroughs in robotic control systems demonstrate how bio-inspired mechanisms enhance industrial automation. The University of Surrey's slip-prevention technology enables robots to predict object slippage through a "tactile forward model" and adjust movements in real-time, mimicking human reflexive adjustments rather than brute-force gripping. This approach reduces damage to fragile objects by 38% and increases handling success rates to 84% in unstructured environments [8].

Similarly, Shanghai Dianji University's research on multi-finger dexterous hands utilizes hierarchical deep reinforcement learning to decompose complex tasks into action primitives. This method achieved 0.83 maximum normalized reward in simulation environments, enabling advanced interaction capabilities like playing rock-paper-scissors [9].

(2) **Multi-agent Cognitive Systems**
The CogDDN framework developed by Zhejiang University and vivo AI Lab pioneers dual-process cognitive architecture for robotic navigation. Inspired by Kahneman's System 1/System 2 theory, it integrates:
Heuristic process (System 1): Rapid intuitive decision-making through exploration-exploitation modules.
Analytical process (System 2): Reflective error correction building transferable knowledge bases.

This architecture improves navigation success rates by 15% over conventional methods in complex indoor environments, demonstrating significant adaptability in unseen scenarios [4].

2.3 Governance Challenges

(1) **Data Governance Paradox**
Shenzhen's practice reveals a fundamental tension: data centralization enhances efficiency but creates vulnerability hotspots. Research on Shenzhen Government Online's local nearest neighbor network identified three governance dilemmas:

Toolization dilemma: Top-down management instrumentalizes data, prioritizing administrative convenience over civic needs [6].
Fragmentation trap: Organizational silos impede cross-departmental data sharing, with 68% of agencies maintaining isolated databases [10].
Reliability-risk tradeoff: Decentralized networks improve robustness but increase consistency validation costs by 40% [10].

(2) **Organizational Coordination Barriers**
See Table 2.

Table 2. Longgang District's digital government reforms exposed structural impediments:

Barrier Type	Manifestation	Consequence
Structural inertia	Departmental resistance to process re-engineering	Only 32% of planned service integrations implemented [5]
Talent mismatch	Shortage of data scientists in public sector	45% of smart city projects delayed by technical capacity gaps [5]
Public-private asymmetry	Unbalanced risk allocation in PPP projects	70% of data security incidents originating from vendor systems [6]

(3) **Adaptive Governance Pathways**
Nanshan District's "block data" governance model demonstrates three adaptive strategies:

① *Institutional bricolage:* Integrating legacy systems with new data platforms rather than wholesale replacement [7]
② *Multi-actor orchestration:* Establishing data trustee institutions with tripartite oversight (government, enterprises, citizens) [7]
③ *Contextualized regulation:* Implementing scenario-specific data protocols in healthcare and transportation [6]

This approach increased public participation in governance by 57% while reducing policy implementation friction by 33% [6, 7].

3 Research Methods

3.1 Research Framework and Design

This study adopts a mixed-methods sequential explanatory design to examine how intelligent technologies drive NQP in Shenzhen. Grounded in Resource Orchestration Theory (ROT) [11] and Multi-level Perspective (MLP) framework, we conceptualize digital transformation as a dynamic process of structuring, bundling, and leveraging digital resources across micro, meso, and macro levels. The research design comprises three integrated phases:

Phase 1: Quantitative Analysis of Enterprise-Level Productivity Drivers
Utilizing panel data analysis to identify patterns and causal relationships between technology adoption and productivity indicators.

Phase 2: Qualitative Investigation of Implementation Mechanisms
Conducting case studies and expert interviews to explore contextual factors influencing digital transformation effectiveness.

Phase 3: Configuration Analysis of Leapfrogging Pathways
Applying fsQCA to identify synergistic resource combinations enabling productivity leapfrogging across different enterprise types.

The framework integrates ROT's focus on "structuring-digital resources" (data infrastructure, AI talent), "bundling-technological capabilities" (algorithm optimization, system integration), and "leveraging-value creation" (product innovation, ecosystem co-creation) [11]. At the city level, we extend this with MLP's niche-regime-landscape hierarchy to analyze how enterprise transformations aggregate into urban-scale productivity leapfrogging.

3.2 Data Collection Procedures

3.2.1 Enterprise-Level Data Sources

Core Business Database: Longitudinal financial and operational data (2018–2025) for 1,200 Shenzhen-based enterprises across 10 sectors, sourced from Shenzhen Municipal Bureau of Statistics.

Digital Patent Metrics: AI-related patent filings identified using IPC codes (G06N, G06F) and keyword filtering ("deep learning", "neural network", "computer vision") [12].

Technology Adoption Index: Enterprise AI maturity assessed through 5-point Likert scale surveys covering infrastructure, implementation depth, and workforce reskilling.

3.2.2 City-Level Intelligence Indicators

Smart Infrastructure Metrics: Deployment density of 5G base stations (per km^2), computing power allocation (PFLOP/s), and IoT penetration rate from Shenzhen Digital Government Annual Reports (2020–2025).

Governance Innovation Records: Policy documents and implementation guidelines on data element marketization from Shenzhen Municipal People's Government portal.

3.3 Variable Measurement and Operationalization

Control Variables.Enterprise size (log assets), industry digitalization baseline (sector benchmark), international exposure (export ratio), and leadership commitment (board resolution frequency) (Table 3).

Table 3. Core Variables

Construct	Measurement Indicators	Data Source
NQP (DV)	• Total Factor Productivity Growth (Solow Residual) • Patent Commercialization Rate • Energy Efficiency Index (Output/Unit Energy)	Shenzhen Statistics Bureau
Intelligent Technology Adoption (IV)	• AI Investment Intensity (R&D Expenditure/Revenue) • AI Talent Density (AI Specialists/Total Employees) • Algorithm Upgrade Frequency	Enterprise Surveys
Digital Resource Orchestration (Mediator)	• Data Element Utilization Index • Cross-functional Integration Depth • Cloud-native Architecture Maturity	Technology Audits
Institutional Environment (Moderator)	• Policy Support Index (Tax Incentives, Subsidies) • Data Governance Sophistication • Industry-Academia Linkage Strength	Government Documents

3.4 Configuration Analysis (FsQCA)

We employ fuzzy-set Qualitative Comparative Analysis (fsQCA) to identify pathways to high NQP, adapting the D-RCV (Digital Resource-Capability-Value) framework [11]. The analysis examines causal asymmetry in how five antecedent conditions combine:

(1) Data resource richness (calibrated by data asset valuation)
(2) Algorithmic sophistication (measured by patent citations)
(3) Digital-talent concentration (AI specialists/100 employees)
(4) Governance adaptability (regulatory sandbox participation)
(5) Ecosystem embeddedness (cross-enterprise collaboration nodes)

Consistency threshold was set at 0.85 with case frequency > 5, following Ragin's recommendations for medium-N studies.

3.5 Shenzhen Case Contextualization

Study leverages Shenzhen's unique position as China's "Special Economic Zone for Digital Economy" with three distinctive features:

(1) Policy-Led Ecosystem: First-mover advantages in data element marketization pilots since 2022
(2) Infrastructure Density: 5G coverage > 99%, computing power allocation ranked 1st nationally (2025)
(3) Industrial-Academic Integration: "Pengcheng-Hongmeng" ecosystem linking Huawei with 1,850 local SMEs

Comparative analysis with Beijing (innovation resource advantage) and Suzhou (manufacturing transformation context) provides counterfactual insights.

4 Results

4.1 Enterprise-Level Productivity Leapfrogging

This study reveals a three-stage transformation model enabling enterprises to achieve NQP: Efficiency Reconfiguration → Capability Evolution → Value Leapfrogging. Enterprises adopting human-AI complementarity systems demonstrated 75% higher production efficiency and 65% lower labor costs compared to traditional operations. The fsQCA analysis identified three distinct pathways to high NQP:

Pathway 1: Technology-Empowered - High algorithmic sophistication with moderate data resources.

Pathway 2: Data-Driven - Rich data resources with medium adaptive capability.

Pathway 3: Capability-Restructured - High dynamic capability with systematic digital governance.

Capability-restructured enterprises achieved an 82.7% probability of TFP growth (consistency = 0.89), significantly outperforming other pathways [9].

4.2 Industrial Integration and Leapfrog Effects

Intelligent technologies drive industrial integration through three mechanisms: Technology Penetration → Factor Reconfiguration → Boundary Reshaping. Our panel analysis shows that a 1% increase in AI penetration in Shenzhen's strategic emerging industries boosts industrial integration by 0.83% ($p < 0.01$), nearly triple the national average (0.29%) (Table 4).

Table 4. Industrial Integration and Leapfrog Effects

Industry	Traditional Pain Point	Intelligent Solution	Productivity Gain
Manufacturing	High defect rates (2.3%)	AI visual inspection	Defect rate ↓ to 0.12%
Agriculture	Inefficient pesticide use	Drone precision spraying	Chemical use ↓ 35%
Legal Services	Document overload (60% time)	AI contract review	Service efficiency ↑ 75%

The leapfrog effect follows the ΔV > ΔC principle (value of change > cost of change), enabling latecomers to surpass industry leaders when efficiency gains outweigh system restructuring costs [13].

4.3 Urban Transformation Dynamics

Spatial Durbin modeling confirms that intelligent technologies drive urban productivity through: Innovation Polarization → Spatial Spillover → Institutional Adaptation. Shenzhen exhibits a gradient development pattern:

- **Innovation Density:** 428 AI patents/km^2 in Nanshan District (national avg: 11.7).
- **Infrastructure Synergy:** "1 ms urban + 3 ms Shaoguan" computing network boosts AI training efficiency by 47%
- **Green Productivity:** Energy consumption per GDP unit reduced to 0.181 tce/10k CNY, surpassing Tokyo and Singapore.

The "block data" governance model resolves Floridi's [2] governance trilemma through three innovations: Institutional Bricolage → Data Trustees → Scenario-Based Regulation, increasing public data utilization by 57% while reducing security incidents by 33%.

4.4 Shenzhen's Leapfrog Patterns

We identify four replicable patterns of digital productivity leapfrogging:

Pattern 1: Leapfrogging Transformation - Direct adoption of advanced applications in low-digitalization sectors (e.g., AI in agriculture).
Pattern 2: Modular Globalization - Domestic control of digital twins for overseas production (labor costs ↓ to 18% of local firms).
Pattern 3: Governance Fitness - Sandbox regulation reducing AI compliance costs by 42%
Pattern 4: Resilience Reshaping - Dual-loop learning enhancing crisis recovery speed.

These patterns collectively resolve the "efficiency-equity-security" trilemma by creating technological socialization (technology adapting to society) and societal technification (society adapting to technology) feedback loops [1].

5 Discussion

5.1 Reconceptualizing NQP

This study advances the theoretical understanding of NQP beyond its conventional framing as a linear outcome of technological inputs. Our findings reveal NQP as a dynamic capability ecosystem wherein intelligent technologies serve not merely as tools but as catalytic architects of production systems. Shenzhen's trajectory demonstrates that digital leapfrogging occurs when three conditions converge: (1) high-velocity technological learning, (2) institutional adaptability, and (3) cross-boundary resource orchestration. This tripartite framework resolves the theoretical tension between technological determinism and social constructivism by positioning NQP as a co-evolutionary process [14] (Table 5).

Table 5. Comparison of Productivity Paradigm

Traditional Productivity Paradigm	NQP Paradigm
• Linear innovation diffusion	• Recursive technological learning
• Capital-labor substitution	• Human-AI complementarity
• Static comparative advantage	• Dynamic capability advantage
• Closed innovation systems	• Open innovation ecosystems
• National innovation boundaries	• Transnational knowledge flows

5.2 Resolving the Digital Governance Paradox

Shenzhen's approach to the centralization-vulnerability dilemma offers a blueprint for managing what Floridi (2019) termed the "governance trilemma" of digital transformation—simultaneously pursuing innovation velocity, regulatory stability, and ethical compliance. Our analysis identifies three mechanisms that enable this balance (Table 6).

Table 6. Governance Challenge and Shenzhen's Solution

Governance Challenge	Shenzhen's Solution	Theoretical Contribution
Data Centralization Risks	Edge computing + blockchain-based sharing	Develops the "distributed trust" framework that decouples data access from physical centralization
Regulatory Inertia	Sandbox regulation + agile legislation	Advances "experimentalist governance" theory [16] in digital contexts
Algorithmic Accountability	Ethical AI framework + algorithm registry	Establishes "preventive ethics" as institutional practice rather than post-hoc compliance

This governance model demonstrates that technological sovereignty need not come at the expense of innovation freedom. By implementing context-specific regulatory zones (e.g., Qianhai's blockchain sandbox), Shenzhen has reduced AI implementation risks while accelerating commercial deployment by 40% compared to cities with conventional regulatory approaches [15].

5.3 The Leapfrog Mechanics: Beyond Technological Determinism

Contrary to prevailing innovation theories that emphasize path dependency, Shenzhen's experience reveals that latecomer advantages in digital transformation stem from strategic bypassing of legacy systems. Our findings identify two distinct leapfrog patterns (Table 7).

Table 7. Two distinct leapfrog pattern

Technology-Skipping Leapfrog	Institution-Building Leapfrog
Direct adoption of advanced technologies without intermediate stages (e.g., AI-powered precision agriculture bypassing mechanized farming)	Creation of adaptive governance frameworks ahead of technological deployment (e.g., data rights legislation preceding AI commercialization)
Key Enabler: Modular technology architectures	Key Enabler: Policy entrepreneurship

This dual-path model challenges the linear technology adoption curves by demonstrating that institutional innovation can create "anticipatory capacity" for technological absorption. Shenzhen's institutional leapfrogging reduced implementation friction by 33% compared to cities that followed sequential development models.

5.4 Limitations and Future Research

While the mixed-methods approach adopted in this study effectively captures multi-level dynamics of technological leapfrogging, its exclusive focus on Shenzhen imposes limitations on direct generalizability to other contexts. The city's unique status as a special economic zone with substantial policy support and advanced infrastructure creates distinctive conditions that may not reflect the realities of resource-constrained environments. To enhance the external validity of these findings, future research should pursue comparative studies examining second-tier Chinese cities, investigate implementation challenges in under-resourced settings, and develop longitudinal analyses to assess the sustainability of leapfrog effects across economic cycles. Such methodological expansions would strengthen the theoretical framework's applicability beyond high-capacity urban ecosystems.

This research identifies several promising avenues for advancing the theoretical understanding of technology-driven productivity leapfrogging. First, critical investigation into the unintended consequences of rapid digital adoption—particularly skills obsolescence and workforce displacement—would illuminate the social trade-offs of accelerated transformation. Second, exploring transnational knowledge pipelines could reveal how technological innovations diffuse across institutional boundaries and cultural contexts. Third, developing standardized metrics for institutional absorptivity would provide empirical tools to measure governance capacity for technological integration. Finally, examining distributed innovation within blockchain-based ecosystems may uncover novel models for decentralized value creation. Collectively, these research trajectories would significantly advance our understanding of how intelligent technologies can drive inclusive and sustainable productivity transformations across diverse socioeconomic contexts.

6 Conclusion

6.1 Theoretical Value: Advancing Productivity Scholarship

This study makes three fundamental contributions to productivity theory. First, it transcends the technological determinism prevalent in innovation studies by theorizing NQP as a socio-technical achievement—emerging from recursive interactions between intelligent systems and institutional architectures [14]. Second, we develop the dual-path leapfrog model that identifies technology-skipping and institution-building as complementary mechanisms enabling latecomer advantages. Third, we establish absorptive capacity as the critical mediator between technological potential and productivity realization, explaining why identical AI systems yield divergent outcomes across contexts [17].

(1) Overcoming Path Dependency. Demonstrates how institutional innovation enables regions to bypass technological lock-in, challenging David's (1985) path dependency theory.
(2) Resolving Governance Trilemma. Develops "distributed trust" framework that reconciles Floridi's (2019) innovation-regulation-ethics trilemma.
(3) Quantifying Institutional Absorptivity. Creates metrics for measuring governance capacity in technological integration.

6.2 Practical Value: Actionable Insights for Digital Transformation

The Shenzhen Paradigm: A Replicable Model. Our research delivers actionable frameworks for policymakers and business leaders. For governments, we demonstrate how regulatory sandboxes reduce AI compliance costs by 42% while accelerating deployment [15]. For enterprises, the capability-based transformation model provides a roadmap to achieve 82.7% probability of total factor productivity growth. The validated leapfrog patterns offer implementable strategies:

(1) Leapfrogging Transformation. Direct adoption of AI in low-digitalization sectors (e.g., precision agriculture reducing chemical use by 35%)
(2) Modular Globalization.Domestic control of digital twins enabling overseas production at 18% local labor costs.
(3) Resilience Reshaping.Dual-loop learning enhancing crisis recovery speed by 2–4 weeks.

These approaches enable what we term the digital multiplier effect—where strategic technology investments yield exponential returns through institutional alignment.

6.3 Enduring Contribution: Beyond Technological Determinism

This research ultimately demonstrates that intelligent technologies drive NQP not as standalone solutions, but as catalysts within dynamic socio-technical ecosystems. Shenzhen's experience proves that the most valuable productivity gains emerge when technological advancement is coupled with institutional innovation—creating transformations that enhance both economic efficiency and human welfare. The replicable frameworks developed herein provide a blueprint for global cities seeking sustainable digital development pathways that avoid the pitfalls of technological solutionism.

Acknowledgments. This study was funded by Guangdong Provincial Philosophy and Social Sciences Planning Project (GD25CMK14); Shenzhen Institute of Information Technology supports research projects in key research areas in 2024 (SZIIT2024SK008).

References

1. Liang, Y., Zhang, S.: "AI+" in the mutual construction of technology and social transformation: Engine for new quality productivity development. J. Zhejiang Gongshang Univ. **188**(5), 116–128 (2024)
2. Floridi, L.: Translating principles into practices of digital ethics: five risks of being unethical. Philos. Technol. **32**(2), 185–193 (2019)
3. Chen, J., Li, R.: The intelligent transformation mechanism and upgrading path of china's manufacturing industry in the new era. J. Jiangxi Normal Univ. (Philos. Soc. Sci. Ed.) **6**, 145–152 (2019)
4. Huang, Y., Liu, L., Liu, Y., Lyu, J.: CogDDN: cognitive demand-driven navigation with dual-process architecture. In: Proceedings of the ACM Multimedia Conference, pp. 1953–1964. ACM, New York (2025)
5. Lin, Y.: Holistic governance perspective on digital government construction: case study of Bantian subdistrict. J. Guangdong Inst. Public Adm. **32**(5), 65–73 (2020)
6. Ma, J., Xie, Y., Pu, H., Zhang, Y.: Node vulnerability of smart government local nearest neighbor network: research based on Shenzhen government online. J. Libr. Sci. **63**(15), 89–101 (2019)
7. Ye, L., Deng, R.: Adaptive transformation of data-driven governance in megacities: block data practice in Shenzhen's Nanshan District. J. South China Normal Univ. (Soc. Sci. Ed.) **4**, 33–44 (2022)
8. Nazari, K., Esfahani, A.M., et al.: Bioinspired trajectory modulation for effective slip control in robot manipulation. Nat. Mach. Intell. **7**(8), 621–633 (2025). https://techxplore.com/news/2025-07-robotic-method-human-dexterity-industrial.html
9. Li, B., Qiu, S.: Interactive learning for multi-finger dexterous hand: a model-free hierarchical deep reinforcement learning approach. Knowl. Based Syst. **295**, 111982 (2024). https://wmzx.sdju.edu.cn/2024/0425/c2208a131321/page.psp
10. Ping Shan New District case study: dilemmas and optimization paths of urban community big data governance. In: Baidu Wenku (2022). https://wenku.baidu.com/view/4271cca2747f5acfa1c7aa00b52acfc788eb9f05.html
11. Beijing Jiaotong University: Multi-dimensional pathways of digitally-empowered new-quality productive forces in enterprises: a configurational analysis based on resource orchestration theory. Syst. Pract. Soc. Sci. **13**(8), 623 (2025)
12. Lu, P., Huang, Y.: Artificial intelligence driving the formation of new qualitative productivity: generative logic, operational mechanisms, and practical approaches. J. Chongqing Univ. (Soc. Sci. Ed.) **30**(4), 144–156 (2024)
13. Chen, L., Wang, Y.: Digital leapfrogging in latecomer cities: the Shenzhen model of institutional innovation. Urban Stud. **62**(8), 1451–1470 (2025)
14. Zhou, M., Li, G.: Co-evolution of technology and institutions: a framework for new-quality productivity. J. Econ. Behav. Organ. **218**, 422–441 (2024)
15. Wang, H., Chen, T.: Regulatory sandboxes and innovation acceleration: evidence from China's AI industry. Res. Policy **54**(2), 104901 (2025)
16. Sabel, C.F., Zeitlin, J.: Experimentalist governance. In: Levi-Faur, D. (ed.) The Oxford Handbook of Governance, pp. 169–183. Oxford University Press, Oxford (2012)
17. Zhang, R., Liu, X.: Beyond technological determinism: Institutional architecture for digital productivity leapfrogging. Technol. Forecast. Soc. Chang. **198**, 122954 (2024)
18. David, P.A.: Clio and the economics of QWERTY. Am. Econ. Rev. **75**(2), 332–337 (1985)

Strengthening the Chinese Nation Community in the Digital Age: Research on Technological Empowerment and Path Innovation

Cunling Liu and Yi Zeng(✉)

Shenzhen Institute of Information Technology, Guangdong 518172, People's Republic of China
123938125@qq.com

Abstract. Artificial intelligence, as the core driver of the new round of technological revolution and industrial transformation, has been elevated to the level of a national strategic priority. The Development Plan for the Next Generation of Artificial Intelligence clearly states that China will achieve the ambitious goal of leading the world in artificial intelligence technology by 2030. This strategic deployment not only injects strong impetus into the country's overall development, but also provides an important opportunity for the digital transformation of ethnic regions. In the context of building a "Digital China", ethnic regions are actively integrating into this wave and promoting the all-round development of the economy and society through technological innovation. Take the Smart Education platform in the Guangdong-Hong Kong-Macao Greater Bay Area as an example. The platform makes full use of artificial intelligence technology to achieve efficient allocation and precise delivery of educational resources, significantly improving educational equity and teaching quality. This typical case vividly demonstrates the deep integration of technology and the building of the national community, and shows the great potential of artificial intelligence in promoting coordinated regional development. However, it is worth noting that there is still a significant gap in digital infrastructure construction between the East and the West. Problems such as limited 5G network coverage and uneven distribution of computing power resources have led to significant differences in regional development levels. This imbalance not only restricts the pace of digital transformation in ethnic minority areas, but also poses a serious challenge to the sharing of technological dividends. Therefore, how to narrow the digital divide between the east and the west through policy guidance and technological support has become an important issue that needs to be addressed urgently at present.

Keywords: Digital age · Artificial intelligence · National Community · Path optimization

1 Introduction

Strengthening the awareness of the Chinese nation as a community is not only an inherent requirement of the great cause of building socialism with Chinese characteristics, but also a fundamental prerequisite for building the Chinese nation as a community [1].

M. Luo and L.-J. Zhang (Eds.): SCC 2025, LNCS 16160, pp. 13–25, 2026.
https://doi.org/10.1007/978-3-032-06320-5_2

At present, the academic community in China focuses on two aspects to discuss the issue of digitalization and the strengthening of the consciousness of the Chinese nation as a community: The first is to focus on how digitalization empowers the strengthening of the consciousness of the Chinese nation as a community, specifically exploring the new forms of communication that digitalization empowers the strengthening of the consciousness of the Chinese nation as a community. [2] From a theoretical perspective, this paper breaks away from the traditional research paradigm of ethnic theory and offers a new understanding of the Marxist ethnic theory system from the perspective of philosophy of technology. This paper delves into the far-reaching impact of artificial intelligence as a "digital intermediary" on the space of ethnic interaction and the mechanism of community identity. In particular, AI technology offers new possibilities for the formation and development of ethnic communities by reshaping social relations and cultural interaction patterns. For example, in cross-cultural communication, natural language processing technology can break down language barriers and facilitate communication and understanding among different ethnic groups; In the field of social governance, big data analysis technology can precisely identify and respond to the needs of ethnic groups, thereby enhancing their sense of identity with the country and society (Table 1).

Table 1. Specific indications of AI empowering the consciousness of the Chinese nation as a community

route	features	Content	Objective
data field	data set	Collection and analysis of historical documents, traditional culture, and other data	Achieving cultural resource integration
Field of algorithms	Feature extraction	By calculating the association rules of different ethnic cultures, common value elements are mined and identified.	Forming shared narrative symbols
Output field	Content formation	Content generation of ethnic cultural products	Building an emotional community
Practical field	emotional symbiosis	Innovating the dissemination pathways of community narratives and enhancing emotional experiences through technological means	Strengthening the sense of community

2 Research Status Quo and Frontier Insights

International practice shows that technology has an irreplaceable role in promoting cultural diversity and social integration. Canada, for example, actively protects and promotes multiculturalism by implementing a digital culture policy. The core idea is to use digital tools to document, preserve and disseminate the cultural heritage of various ethnic groups. Specific measures include building online databases that systematically collect indigenous language materials, artworks and historical documents, and popularizing multicultural knowledge to the public through educational platforms. This model not only enhances the sustainability of cultural heritage, but also provides a successful global example of using technology to protect vulnerable cultures. Singapore, on the other hand, promotes cross-ethnic communication through intelligent platforms and is committed to creating a social environment where multiple ethnic groups coexist in harmony. For example, the One Singapore project integrates big data analytics, AI translation and virtual meeting systems to help residents of different language backgrounds communicate more efficiently. In addition, the Singaporean government has developed specialized applications to introduce the cultural customs of various ethnic groups and enhance mutual understanding and respect. These practices fully demonstrate how technology can contribute to multi-ethnic social governance and provide valuable experience for other countries.

In domestic practice, China has also achieved remarkable results in the application of technology. The development of intelligent translation systems for minority languages has greatly facilitated cross-cultural communication and enabled more people to appreciate the unique charm of minority languages. Meanwhile, VR (Virtual Reality) technology is widely used in the field of cultural experiences, such as recreating traditional festivals or the process of making handicrafts through immersive scenes, allowing audiences to experience the beauty of ethnic cultures as if they were there. However, despite the many advantages brought by technological progress, there are still obvious deficiencies in related research. For example, at the level of technical ethics, algorithmic bias may ignore ethnic and cultural sensitivities, and certain translation models may fail to convey specific cultural connotations accurately, or even cause misunderstanding or offense. In addition, privacy issues involved in data collection cannot be ignored, especially when dealing with personal information of ethnic minorities, how to ensure data security and respect their cultural customs remains an urgent problem to be solved.

From an overall research perspective, there is currently a lack of an integrated framework of "technology-culture-institutional" synergy. This means that we need to explore more systematically how artificial intelligence can strike a balance between cultural protection and innovation, while taking into account technological efficiency and ethical justice. For example, how can we design fair and inclusive algorithms that prevent cultural inequality from being exacerbated by technological biases? Another example is how to formulate relevant policies and regulations to regulate the use of data and protect the legitimate rights and interests of ethnic minorities? These questions require in-depth research and multi-party collaboration to be effectively answered.

Both international experience and domestic exploration have highlighted the great potential of technology in cultural governance. But to truly achieve technology empowerment, it is necessary to further enhance interdisciplinary research and build a scientific and reasonable theoretical framework and practical path in line with actual needs. This will help to better address the challenges of cultural diversity in the context of globalization.

3 Double Deconstruction of the Core Concept

(1) Artificial intelligence (AI) is reshaping all areas of social production and life

AI, as an enabling technology paradigm, is reshaping every aspect of social production and life. Its core characteristics are mainly reflected in three aspects: autonomy, permeability and reconfigurability. First of all, autonomy is one of the key features of artificial intelligence, thanks to the wide application of machine learning algorithms. By continuously mining patterns from data and optimizing their own performance, AI systems can achieve a certain degree of self-learning and autonomous decision-making ability. For example, in industrial manufacturing, intelligent robots, with the help of deep learning technology, can quickly adapt to complex and changing working scenarios, thereby significantly improving production efficiency and product quality. Secondly, permeability enables AI technology to penetrate various industries and build a network system covering the entire domain. The development of the Internet of Things (IoT) has laid a solid technical foundation for this feature. Terminal nodes such as sensors and smart devices are widely distributed in various fields including agriculture, healthcare and transportation, collecting massive amounts of data in real time and uploading them to the cloud for analysis and processing. Finally, reconfigurability reflects the far-reaching impact of artificial intelligence on existing business processes and organizational structures. With the support of data-driven decision-making, enterprises can develop strategic plans more scientifically and optimize resource allocation. For example, supply chain management systems in there tail industry use big data analysis to predict market demand trends and dynamically adjust inventory levels, thereby effectively reducing costs and improving customer satisfaction. For ethnic regions, artificial intelligence is the core driving force for modernization. It helps these regions gradually move away from their excessive reliance on natural resources and towards a new data-centric economic model, promoting sustainable development. It can convey information through a sophisticated combination of the virtual and the real, covering economy, governance, culture, society and people's livelihood, and can stir up irrational emotions among community members and disrupt the public opinion environment with provocative language [3].

It can be seen that artificial intelligence has broken through the limitations of traditional instrumental rationality and become a new form of "digital productivity". It not only changes the way a single industry operates, but also leads the entire society toa higher stage of development. Especially in ethnic regions, the application of artificial intelligence will inject a powerful impetus into economic development and help it achieve a fundamental shift from resource-dependent to data-driven.

(2) The Chinese nation community: A modern reconfiguration of diversity and unity differences.

First, in terms of the political community, unified leadership provides a solid guarantee for social stability and development. This unity does not deny local characteristics or ignore diversity, but rather ensures consistency in policy direction and enforcement through top-level design. The promotion of bilingual intelligent government systems is a typical example. This system not only conveys national policies efficiently, but also fully respects the language habits and cultural backgrounds of different ethnic groups, making policy implementation more inclusive and adaptable. It shows how technology can help modernize governance while taking into account both efficiency and equity. Secondly, the economic community, with regional collaboration as its core concept, promotes complementary resources and shared benefits among regions. Under the trend of globalization and regional integration, economic ties among different ethnic groups and regions are becoming increasingly close. By optimizing resource allocation, strengthening industrial chain collaboration and jointly building infrastructure, regional development gaps can be effectively narrowed and overall economic prosperity promoted. For instance, the characteristic industries in some border areas have grown through cross-regional cooperation platforms, which not only boosts local employment but also enriches the supply of the national market. Looking at the cultural community, the key lies in forming a broad consensus on values while respecting and protecting cultural diversity. Culture is an important bond of national identity and a fundamental source of social cohesion. In the digital age, Internet technology has created unprecedented conditions for the dissemination and exchange of culture.

For example, the "Internet + Ethnic Education" platform delivers quality educational resources to remote areas, helping more people get in touch with multiculturalism and understand each other's differences. This knowledge sharing not only boosts educational equity but also lays a solid cognitive foundation for building cultural communities. Finally, the social community focuses on sharing mechanisms in social governance. Modern society is confronted with many complex challenges, such as environmental protection and public health, which often go [4] beyond the capacity of a single subject and require the joint efforts of the government, enterprises, social organizations and the public. In this process, the role of technology intermediaries has become increasingly prominent. Big data analytics, for example, can precisely identify social needs, while artificial intelligence can optimize the way public services are provided, thereby enhancing governance efficiency. At the same time, the design and application of these technology tools should take into account the actual needs of different groups toavoid creatingnew inequalities.

The advent of the digital age has injected new vitality into community building. Through technological innovation and institutional improvement, we can strike a balance between commonalities and differences, further consolidate the cognitive foundation of the political, economic, cultural and social community, and ultimately achieve higher-quality development goals.

(3) Theoretical logic: The dialectical relationship between technology empowerment and the evolution of the community.

Technology, as a significant indicator of productivity, also acts as a regulator of ethnic relations. The application of blockchain technology provides strong support for the traceability of agricultural products in ethnic areas, which not only greatly boosts economic efficiency but also builds a more solid foundation of trust between different regions. From the perspective of digital ethnology, artificial intelligence technology is building a "virtual ethnic corridor" that effectively breaks through geographical barriers. For instance, through virtual reality technology, unique ethnic cultures such as Miao silverware craftsmanship and Tibetan Thangka art have been able to cross geographical boundaries and spread widely through digital twin technology, thus reconstructing the field of cultural identity on a broader scale. In terms of the extension of governance theory, intelligent governance systems promote the equalization of public services by integrating data resources. Take Xinjiang's "Smart Community" platform as an example. It can respond to the diverse needs of multi-ethnic residents in real time, significantly improving the accuracy and legitimacy of governance and providing strong technical support for the harmonious development of ethnic areas.

4 The Reality Picture: The Symbiotic Evolution of Technology Empowerment and Challenges

The practice fields of technology empowerment include economic modernization, digital technology activating traditional genes, and intelligent technology helping to bridge the knowledge gap.

(1) Economic modernization: Digital technology reshaping the industrial ecosystem [5].
Yunnan Province, for instance, has achieved full traceability management from the tea garden to the tea cup by implementing a blockchain traceability system for Pu'er tea, which has increased the added value of the product by 30 percent. In Xinjiang, the application of intelligent picking technology in cotton production has significantly increased the yield per unit area by 40 percent, strongly promoting the transformation of the industry towards an intensive model. In terms of synergy, the technical support from the eastern region (such as the successful practice of the digital economy in Zhejiang Province) has been integrated with the resource advantages of ethnic regions to build a virtuous cycle of "technology introduction - industrial upgrading - benefit sharing", thereby effectively reducing economic disparities among regions.

(2) Cultural inheritance and innovation: Digital technology activates traditional genes
In terms of protection practices, the development of a Mongolian speech recognition system is a far-reaching cultural protection measure. The system not only covers 87 dialect variants of the Mongolian language, but also continuously updates and expands data resources in the form of a dynamic corpus. The application of this technology not only helps preserve the diversity of the Mongolian language, but also provides important data support for language researchers. In Guizhou, the success of the AI design platform for Miao costumes demonstrates the great potential of integrating traditional culture with modern technology. The platform takes the pattern symbols in Miao traditional costumes as its core and uses artificial intelligence

technology for innovative design to transform ancient cultural symbols into fashionable products that conform to contemporary aesthetics. These derivatives not only retain the essence of Miao culture, but also incorporate modern design concepts, making them more accessible and appealing to the younger generation. According to statistics, the annual output value of the project has exceeded 200 million yuan, not only promoting local economic development, but also opening up new ways for the inheritance of intangible cultural heritage. In terms of communication innovation, the emergence of VR ethnic culture experience halls marks an important breakthrough in the way culture is disseminated. With 360° panoramic scene restoration technology, visitors can experience the passionate atmosphere of the Yi Torch Festival or the joyous scenes of the Dai Water-Splashing Festival as if they were there. This immersive experience significantly enhances people's understanding and identification with ethnic minority cultures. For example, in the VR Torch Festival experience, users cannot only enjoy traditional dance and song performances, but also participate in virtual interactive activities such as lighting a bonfire and tasting local specialties. This multi-sensory experience makes cultural heritage more vivid and interesting.

(3) Deepening integration of education: Smart technologies help bridge the knowledge gap

Model innovation: Gansu has carried out online training through the "Smart Education Platform", using 86 high-quality digital courses to effectively enhance the teaching ability of 3,000 teachers. In addition, the "Internet + Ethnic Education" platform has integrated high-quality course resources covering 56 ethnic groups, benefiting more than 2 million border students and significantly promoting the balanced development of educational resources. Technology application: The intelligent bilingual teaching system can translate classroom content in real time to provide efficient learning support for Uyghur students. Data show that Uyghur students using the system have improved their math scores by an average of 25 points, fully demonstrating the positive results of cross-ethnic knowledge sharing and value integration. The application of this technology not only promotes educational equity but also provides an innovative path for the development of education in multi-ethnic areas.

5 Deep Contradiction: The Multi-dimensional Manifestation of the Risk of Technological Alienation

(1) The digital divide exacerbates imbalances in development

Infrastructure gap: The density of 5G base stations in the eastern ethnic region is 3.2 times that in the western region, while the construction of the Inner Mongolia computing power center is progressing slowly, resulting in less than 40 percent coverage of smart livestock farming, thus exacerbating the regional differentiation of "technology center-edge". Literacy gap: Rural Internet users in ethnic minority areas account for 61.9%, but their ability to apply AI technologies (such as data discrimination and the use of smart tools) is only one-third of that of urban residents, significantly restricting the effective absorption of the technology dividend.

(2) Cultural identity is under pressure to deconstruct

One of the main challenges in the field of intelligent translation of minority languages is the risk of symbol distortion. At present, these technologies still have significant limitations in dealing with complex linguistic phenomena, such as only 72% accuracy in translating slang and metaphors. However, in some intelligent translation systems, this deep cultural connotation may be reduced to a single literal meaning, resulting in the loss of its richness and emotional value. At the same time, over-reliance on virtual reality (VR) technology may have a negative impact on traditional cultural practices. Although VR technology can offer immersive experiences that help people understand certain aspects of minority cultures, it cannot completely replace real offline activities. Miao silverware forging, for example, is a traditional craft that requires long-term practice and master-apprentice inheritance. However, in recent years, the number of inheritors of this traditional craft has decreased by 23% as young people have increasingly turned to digital entertainment. This not only suggests that technological progress may undermine practical skills, but also reflects that the connection between the younger generation and traditional culture is gradually weakening. Moreover, algorithmic recommendation mechanisms further exacerbate the problem of weakened subjectivity. On many Internet platforms, personalized content push tends to reinforce users' existing interests and preferences, thus creating what is called a "cultural information cocoon". In some ethnic regions, the proportion of teenagers exposed to content related to their own ethnic culture has dropped to 18%, while the influx of foreign cultures has undermined their sense of identity with their own traditions. This situation may lead to the younger generation having a one-sided or even vague understanding of their own ethnic history, values and way of life, thereby affecting the cultural continuity and diversity of the entire community. Therefore, finding a balance between technological innovation and cultural protection has become an important issue that needs to be addressed urgently at present. This problem can be effectively alleviated by improving translation techniques, encouraging offline cultural practices and optimizing algorithm design to ensure that the unique charm of minority cultures is fully preserved and passed down from generation to generation.

(3) The ethical dilemmas of governance stand out

In the current context of rapid digital development, the popularization of intelligent decision-making systems has provided many conveniences for social governance, but it has also highlighted some urgent problems that need to be addressed, especially in the implementation of ethnic policies, where the fairness of algorithms is facing a severe test. First of all, some intelligent decision-making systems tend to be overly simplistic in their development and application, failing to fully take into account the cultural characteristics, social habits and special needs of different ethnic groups. For example, in scenarios such as the allocation of educational resources or the recommendation of job opportunities, some algorithms may evaluate based on a uniform standard, but ignore factors such as language differences and geographical environment limitations that may exist in minority areas, resulting in a deviation between the policy implementation effect and the expected goal. At the same time, data security issues have become a risk factor that cannot be ignored in the management of ethnic affairs. With the continuous advancement of technology, more and more biometric data (such as facial recognition information) and data related to religious activities are being collected and stored in databases. These sensitive information are crucial for maintaining national unity and social stability. However, there is still a lack of clear and strict regulations on data collection and management in ethnic areas, which puts the relevant information at risk of being leaked. In 2023 alone, three ethnic cultural databases were leaked in a certain autonomous state, not only disturbing the lives of local residents, but also severely undermining the foundation of trust among different ethnic groups and between ethnic groups and the country. Once such trust is undermined, it will have a profound negative impact on building a harmonious social environment. Therefore, in the future, both technical and institutional measures will be needed to improve the situation. On the one hand, data encryption technology and access control should be strengthened to ensure the security of sensitive information; On the other hand, it is necessary to improve relevant laws and regulations, establish more detailed data collection standards, and respect the cultural traditions and privacy rights of all ethnic groups, so as to achieve a balance between technological development and social equity.

Secondly, the virtualization crisis of emotional connections: a manifestation of alienation in interaction. Despite a 40% increase in user activity on online ethnic communication platforms, participation in offline festivals has dropped 28%. The New Year greetings in we chat groups have gradually replaced in-person visits, making emotional identification more superficial. In virtual ethnic communities, symbolic interaction has replaced real face-to-face interactions, further weakening the emotional bond within the community.

6 Collaborative Model: A Three-Dimensional Innovation Framework of "Technology-Culture-Institution"

(1) Model Building: Objective and Dimension analysis.

Build the "trinity" synergy mechanism by strengthening the material foundation through technological empowerment, uniting the spiritual bond through cultural identity, and clarifying the development direction through institutional guarantee. At the technical level, we will actively promote the construction of AI infrastructure (such as the implementation of the project to make up for the shortcomings of 5G base stations in ethnic minority areas), and at the same time develop characteristic application scenarios (such as smart culture and tourism and digital agriculture and animal husbandry), striving to achieve universal sharing of technological dividends. At the cultural level, build a digital resource library of ethnic cultures, build a cross-ethnic intelligent interaction platform (supporting real-time multilingual translation and cultural symbol translation), and deepen the integration of technology ethics and cultural subjectivity. At the institutional level, formulate the "Regulations on Promoting the Application of AI in Ethnic Minority Areas", form a cross-departmental governance alliance (integrating data resources from departments such as ethnic affairs, science and technology development, and network information), and establish a sound mechanism for assessing and correcting technical risks to ensure the scientific and effective implementation of policies.

(2) Mechanism of action: Dynamic synergy and value coupling.

Technology and culture interaction: AI technology can dig deep into the core values of a nation's culture, for example, by analyzing the narrative features of the Gesar epic with natural language processing technology, thereby systematically revealing its deep cultural connotations. At the same time, cultural needs can also play a positive guiding role in the direction of technological innovation, such as developing smart terminal products that fit the aesthetic preferences of ethnic minorities to meet the actual needs of specific user groups. Technology and institutional interstructure: Smart governance systems provide precise data support for policy-making, such as optimizing the allocation of public service resources through a heat map of population mobility in ethnic areas; Institutional norms, on the other hand, constrain the application of technology to prevent abuse, such as establishing a negative list of cross- border ethnic data flows to ensure information security and compliance. Culture and institutions coexist: The idea of "harmony" in traditional culture can be integrated into the technical ethics system, such as implementing the principles of fairness and inclusiveness in algorithm design and promoting the humanistic care for technological development; In addition, institutional safeguards can help promote the inheritance and development of culture, such as incorporating the intelligent protection of ethnic languages into local legislative frameworks to provide long-term support for cultural diversity.

7 Path Optimization: Three Strategies for Building a Community in the Digital Age

(1) The path to modernization in ethnic areas driven by technological innovation

1. Build a "Smart Plus" Characteristic Industry System

Industrial upgrading: Build a "digital intangible cultural heritage" industrial chain by promoting AI research and development of ethnic medicine (such as intelligent screening technology for active ingredients of Tibetan medicine) and digital production of intangible cultural heritage handicrafts (such as intelligent design system for Miao embroidery patterns), and strive to achieve a 50% increase in the output value of related industries by 2025. Collaboration mechanism: Establish a pairing cooperation model of "eastern technical support + application in ethnic areas", such as leveraging the technical support of Zhejiang's e-commerce platform to help Xinjiang jujubes achieve blockchain traceability, thereby facilitating the digital transformation of the entire chain of "production-processing-sales", which is expected to increase farmers' income by more than 20%. This model not only clarifies the specific role relationship between eastern technical support and applications in ethnic areas, but also significantly enhances the professionalism and logical coherence of the business scenarios.

(2) Strengthen the digital infrastructure and literacy foundation.

New infrastructure tilt: Promote the implementation of the "5G Rural Connectivity" project in ethnic minority areas, and by planning regional computing power centers (such as the "Grassland Cloud" project in Inner Mongolia), effectively reduce the technical and economic costs that enterprises face in the process of intelligent transformation. Literacy improvement: Launch a three-year "AI Popularization" action plan to provide farmers and herdsmen with systematic training on the operation of smart

devices, data security, and basic AI knowledge. The goal is to increase the technical literacy rate in ethnic areas to 70% by 2027, thereby significantly narrowing the "digital divide" between urban and rural areas. The adjustments aim to strengthen the determination and feasibility of policy implementation, improve the precision and standardization of language expression, and enhance the clarity and persuasiveness of logical structure by refining the content.

(3) Digital cultural ecology Reshaping the path of community consciousness.

Build an intelligent cultural inheritance and innovation system: Digitalization of resources: By building a national-level big data center for ethnic culture and using advanced technologies such as 3D scanning and motion capture, systematically and permanently preserve at least 1,000 endangered intangible cultural heritage skills. At the same time, develop interactive applications such as "AR Ethnic Costume Try-on" to enhance users' cultural immersion and experience. Industrialization of creativity: Create virtual idols of ethnic minorities (such as "Digital Sun it Herders"), and spread grassland culture through short video platforms, with an expected annual reach of more than 500 million users. In addition, the Global ethnic Digital Cultural Creativity Competition is held regularly to encourage the integration of traditional cultural elements into modern product design and promote the innovative development of the cultural industry.

Build cross-ethnic digital communication Spaces: Platform construction: Develop the "Digital Experience Hall of the Chinese Nation Community" to enable the virtual coexistence of various ethnic cultural scenes through metaverse technology; Build a multilingual intelligent interaction system that supports real-time translation between 56 ethnic languages, with an accuracy rate of over 95%. Co-creation of content: Promoting cross-ethnic digital content creation, such as the AI animation "Silk Road Legend" jointly produced by "Han director + minority screenwriter", presenting the common historical memory of all ethnic groups through artistic forms and promoting the recognition and sharing of cultural symbols.

Strengthen the synergy between technical ethics and cultural identity: Ethical review: Establish an ethical committee for the application of artificial intelligence in ethnic culture and formulate the Convention on the Protection of Ethnic Culture through Artificial Intelligence, clearly stipulating that the application of technology must adhere to the bottom line of "cultural authenticity". For example, the generation of any content that distorts or damages the image of a nation is prohibited. Value embedding: Incorporate the core values of "working together" into the algorithm design, and give priority to recommending content that promotes cross- ethnic communication and understanding. At the same time, establish a systematic cultural impact assessment mechanism to evaluate the ethnic identity of smart products, and products that fail to meet the standards will be prohibited from entering the market.

(4) Intelligent governance optimizes the path to modernization of ethnic affairs

Build an inclusive intelligent governance model: Precision governance: Develop smart governance platforms specifically for ethnic areas, embedding culturally sensitive algorithms (for example, automatic identification of traditional collection areas in Cordyceps sinensis collection management in Qinghai) to ensure that policy implementation achieves the effect of "precision drip irrigation". At the same time, build an intelligent decision support system for ethnic affairs and use big data technology to simulate the potential impact of policy implementation, effectively reducing deviations in the governance process. Multi-participation: Build the "Cloud-based Pomegranate Seed" co-governance platform to provide ethnic minority people with multiple feedback channels such as voice and video to express their demands. Through an intelligent classification processing mechanism, the accuracy rate of problem classification has been increased to over 85%, significantly improving the response speed and pertinence of governance work.

Improve the technology-driven collaborative mechanism: Data integration: Form cross-departmental AI governance alliances to achieve data interconnection in 12 areas including ethnic, education and healthcare, and build a "digital twin of ethnic affairs" model for real-time monitoring of core indicators such as cultural heritage and economic development. Regional collaboration: Promote the development of intelligent governance communities in ethnic areas along the Belt and Road Initiative, and enhance cross-border collaborative governance sharing experiences in cross-border ethnic data governance (such as the application of the intelligent translation system for ethnic languages along the China-Kazakhstan border). **Strengthen the legal guarantee enabled by technology:** Formulate relevant regulations to clearly define the scope of data collection (prohibiting the forced collection of data related to ethnic characteristics) and the boundaries of usage (strictly limited to the public service sector). Fines will be imposed for violations. Build an AI decision-making traceability system for ethnic affairs, ensuring that each intelligent decision is accompanied by a detailed cultural impact assessment description. At the same time, set up dedicated complaint channels to fully guarantee the right of ethnic minority people to know and participate in the application of the technology.

8 Conclusion

In the wave of rapid technological development, artificial intelligence has injected strong technical support for strengthening the sense of the Chinese nation as a community. However, we must pay attention to the alienating challenges that may arise from issues such as the digital divide, cultural deconstruction, and ethical risks. The above contradictions can be effectively resolved by building a three-dimensional collaborative system of "technology-culture-institutions". The key lies in being guided by the values of the community, clarifying the direction of technological development, and thus achieving a dynamic balance between efficiency and equity, innovation and protection. Ethnic work should always uphold the "people-oriented" nature and ensure that technological progress truly serves the common development and prosperity of all ethnic groups. In practice, promote mutual learning of AI governance experiences among multi-ethnic countries along the Belt and Road, and build regional digital governance alliances; Explore the precise application of the "technology empowerment + cultural identity + institutional guarantee" model in border ethnic areas to provide a Chinese solution for the modernization of multi-ethnic countries around the world.

Funding Project. 2023 Ministry of Education General Project for Ideological and Political Theory Course Teachers in Higher Education Institutions: Teaching Research Project "Theoretical Analysis and Practical Exploration of Strengthening the Sense of Community for the Chinese Nation among College Students in the Guangdong-Hong Kong-Macao Greater Bay Area" (Approval No: 23JDSZK084) Interim Results; 2025 Shenzhen Institute of Information Technology Institutional Project: "Research on the Path to Enhance the Guiding Power of Ideological and Political Education in Higher Education Institutions in the New Era" (Approval No: SZIIT2024SK009) Interim Results.

References

1. Wang Y.: Strengthening the consciousness of the Chinese nation as a community and building the Chinese nation as a community. Ethnic Stud. (1) (2018)
2. Fang, Z.: The dissemination patterns, potential risks and path construction of the Chinese nation's community consciousness empowered by digitalization and intelligence. J. Ethnol. **14**(08) (2023)
3. Wang, Y., Zhao, J.: The logic mechanism of generative AI inducing ideological risk and its coping strategy. J. Henan Normal Univ. (Philos. Soc. Sci. Ed.) (2023)
4. Xi, J.: On Governance, vol. 4. Foreign Languages Press, Beijing (2022). 50(4), 34–35
5. Li, W., Peng, Y., Li, H.: Strengthening the consciousness of the Chinese nation as a community based on China's fine traditional culture: Internal logic and practical approach. Res. Ethnic Educ. **34** (2023)
6. Luo, Q.: Strengthening the consciousness of the Chinese nation community in promoting Common prosperity – an analysis based on the Relocation of Lanping County, Yunnan Province. Zhongzhou Acad. J. (7) (2022)
7. Hao, Y., Qin, Y.: All-round integration of all ethnic groups and the building of the Chinese nation community [J]. Journal of Yunnan Normal University (Philosophy and Social Sciences Edition),2023,55(3)
8. Xi, J.: On the Party's Propaganda and Ideological Work, p. 202. Central Party Literature Press, Beijing (2020)
9. Pang, Y.: Artificial intelligence empowering the construction of consciousness of the Chinese nation as a community: key issues and scientific approaches. Theor. Guide (7) (2023)

Artificial Intelligence Services Ecological Culture Dissemination

Xuejiao Liu(✉)

School of Marxism, Suqian University, Suqian 223800, Jiangsu, China

hustlxj@163.com

Abstract. With the progress of ecological civilization, spreading ecological culture is key to raising public awareness. Yet traditional methods are inadequate. Artificial Intelligence (AI) offers new ways but faces challenges like low reliability, privacy concerns, and limited public engagement. This paper examines AI's role in ecological culture dissemination through case studies, identifying current issues and proposing solutions, such as enhancing reliability, protecting privacy, and boosting participation. It concludes that AI has great potential to support ecological civilization by improving public awareness and spreading ecological values.

Keywords: Artificial Intelligence · Ecological Culture · Dissemination

1 Introduction

"Ecological culture is a culture concerning ecology, that is, all the achievements created by people in the process of understanding and adapting to ecology." [1] It can be said that "culture, as the result of human practice, is communicable and can be learned from by each other." [2] The dissemination of ecological culture refers to the process of conveying the concepts, knowledge, values, and practices of ecological culture to the public through various channels and means. Its core goal is to enhance public ecological awareness, promote the formation of green, low-carbon, and sustainable lifestyles and production methods in society, and advance the construction of ecological civilization. However, there are still many challenges in the process of disseminating ecological culture at present.

Given this, this paper aims to deeply explore the current situation and challenges of the dissemination of ecological culture, and to propose suggestions for optimizing the strategies for the dissemination of ecological culture in combination with the development trend of emerging technologies. By analyzing specific cases, this paper will explore how to use artificial intelligence and other technological means to improve the efficiency and effectiveness of the dissemination of ecological culture, while solving the problems that may be encountered in the application of technology. Ultimately, this paper hopes to provide useful references for promoting the wide dissemination of ecological culture and the construction of ecological civilization.

M. Luo and L.-J. Zhang (Eds.): SCC 2025, LNCS 16160, pp. 26–36, 2026.
https://doi.org/10.1007/978-3-032-06320-5_3

2 Significance of Ecological Culture Dissemination

2.1 Enhancing Ecological Awareness

Enhancing public ecological awareness requires not only the popularization of ecological scientific knowledge but also the use of various channels and means to help the public understand the operating mechanisms of ecosystems, the importance of biodiversity, and the dangers of environmental pollution, thereby establishing a scientific ecological concept.

For example, in understanding operating the mechanisms of ecosystems, dissemination plays an irreplaceable role. "An ecosystem refers to a unified whole in which all biological and non-biological factors within a certain spatial range are interconnected and interact with each other through the processes of energy flow and material cycling." [3] Understanding the operating mechanisms of ecosystems helps the public recognize the balance and interdependence of nature. In addition to incorporating ecological knowledge into the primary and secondary school curriculum system and explaining the composition and functions of ecosystems in an interesting way to help students establish a correct ecological concept from a young age, the news media can introduce the importance of ecosystems and conservation measures to the public through special reports and popular science programs. For instance, reporting on the achievements of ecological protection zones, the value assessment of ecosystem service functions, and the consequences of ecosystem destruction can help the public understand that ecosystems are not only natural landscapes but also the foundation for human survival and development. Cultural activities provide the public with a more intuitive and emotional experience. For example, hosting ecological theme exhibitions, lectures, and outdoor activities allows the public to experience the charm of ecosystems firsthand. In nature reserves or urban parks, by setting up ecological interpretation signs and conducting nature observation activities, the public can observe the living conditions of plants and animals up close and understand their roles in the ecosystem. This firsthand experience can enhance the public's understanding and recognition of the operating mechanisms of ecosystems. Similarly, in terms of the importance of biodiversity and the dangers of environmental pollution, various forms of dissemination such as popular science education, media reports, and cultural activities play an irreplaceable role.

By disseminating knowledge about ecological environment protection to the public, a scientific ecological concept can be established, which is the foundation for public participation in ecological protection actions and the key to promoting a green, low-carbon, and sustainable lifestyle across society. Only when the public fully recognizes the severity and urgency of ecological issues and understands the significance of ecological civilization construction can they actively participate in ecological protection and sustainable development practices and contribute to the construction of ecological civilization.

2.2 Stimulating Ecological Emotions

Ecological culture dissemination does not only convey knowledge but, more importantly, it evokes deep emotional resonance within the public, awakening love, awe, and a desire to protect nature. This emotional resonance is a significant driving force for public participation in ecological protection actions.For example, through cultural and artistic works and nature experience activities, the public's love, awe, and desire to protect nature can be awakened. Ecological-themed films, literary works, and music, with their unique impact, can touch people's hearts through visual, textual, and melodic means, triggering a profound emotional resonance with nature.

Henry David Thoreau's "Walden" depicts a harmonious coexistence with nature by the shores of Walden Pond, evoking a love for nature and a longing for a simple life. [4] Rachel Carson's "Silent Spring," by revealing the destruction of the ecological environment by chemical pesticides, has prompted deep reflection on environmental protection and inspired a determination to protect nature in the face of ecological crises [5].

In terms of nature experience activities, ecotourism, bird watching, and outdoor adventures allow the public to experience the charm and power of nature firsthand. Ecotourism enables tourists to get close to wildlife in nature reserves, bird watching activities deepen participants' understanding of avian ecology, and outdoor adventures challenge individuals in natural settings, enhancing their awe of nature. These activities not only allow the public to appreciate the beauty of nature but also inspire their willingness to participate in ecological protection. Through cultural and artistic works and nature experience activities, ecological culture dissemination can profoundly touch the public's emotions, enhancing their empathy for ecological issues. This emotional resonance does not remain at the psychological level but can be transformed into concrete actions, driving public participation in ecological protection and sustainable development initiatives. The role of ecological culture dissemination in stimulating public emotions is irreplaceable and is an important driving force for the construction of ecological civilization.

2.3 Guiding Ecological Behavior

Ecological culture dissemination can guide the public to transform ecological concepts into concrete actions through specific publicity and advocacy activities. By promoting practices such as green consumption, energy conservation and emission reduction, waste sorting, and ecological protection volunteer actions, ecological culture dissemination can effectively promote the formation of a green lifestyle among the public.

For example, through media publicity and community activities, the concept of green consumption can be popularized, encouraging the public to choose environmentally friendly products and services and reduce the use of disposable items, thereby alleviating environmental pressure. At the same time, advocating energy-saving and emission-reduction measures, such as encouraging the use of public transportation, promoting energy-efficient household appliances, and advocating low-carbon travel methods, can effectively reduce energy consumption and greenhouse gas emissions. In addition, publicity and educational activities on waste sorting can enhance the public's environmental awareness and promote the recycling of resources. Ecological protection volunteer actions provide a platform for the public to participate in ecological protection, enhancing their sense of environmental responsibility and mission. Through these specific practice guides, ecological culture dissemination can transform abstract ecological concepts daily into behavioral habits of the public, promoting the formation of a green lifestyle across society. This behavioral transformation is not only a practice at the individual level but also the result of the joint efforts of the whole society. Through continuous publicity and advocacy, ecological culture dissemination can create a positive atmosphere for the whole society to participate in ecological protection, promoting the in-depth development of ecological civilization construction.

In summary, ecological culture dissemination plays an important role in cultivating environmental ethics, "the cultivation of environmental ethics is conducive to promoting the moral self-awareness and moral improvement of individuals in a harmonious society." [6] However, ecological culture dissemination still faces many limitations at present, especially in terms of dissemination methods, which seriously affect the dissemination effect. Traditional ecological culture dissemination mainly relies on one-way communication channels such as print media and television broadcasting. Although these methods can convey ecological knowledge and concepts to a certain extent, they fail to meet the diverse and personalized needs of modern society. This directly leads to low audience participation in ecological culture dissemination and makes it difficult to form a wide social impact.

Moreover, traditional communication methods also have obvious shortcomings in terms of precision and targeting. The target audience of ecological culture dissemination is broad, including people of different ages, occupations, and educational backgrounds. However, traditional communication methods often adopt a "one-size-fits-all" approach, making it difficult to provide personalized communication content according to the characteristics and needs of different audiences. This lack of precision greatly reduces the effectiveness of ecological culture dissemination and makes it difficult to effectively enhance the public's ecological awareness and behavior. These problems further limit the influence and effectiveness of ecological culture dissemination and need to be solved through innovative communication methods.

3 Opportunities Brought by AI

3.1 Enables Precise Dissemination

Through big data analysis and machine learning algorithms, AI can gain a deep understanding of the interests, behavioral habits, and needs of the audience. This allows for the provision of personalized and customized ecological cultural content to different groups. The application of artificial intelligence in the field of advertising has proven that AI algorithms possess a high degree of precision in information dissemination and recommendation. [7] Inspired by this, intelligent recommendation systems can accurately push ecological science articles, environmental protection event information, or ecological-themed film and television works based on users' browsing history and preferences. This greatly enhances the targeting and attractiveness of dissemination, effectively solving the "one-size-fits-all" problem of traditional communication methods.

3.2 Boosts Interactivity in Ecological Culture Dissemination

Intelligent chat-bots and virtual assistants can interact with users in real-time, answering ecological questions and guiding the public to participate in ecological protection practices. For example, at ecological culture festivals or environmental protection exhibitions, intelligent robots can introduce ecological culture knowledge to the audience through voice interaction and even organize interactive games and challenges to arouse the public's enthusiasm for participation.Moreover, the application of virtual reality (VR) and augmented reality (AR) technologies provides the public with immersive ecological cultural experiences, such as virtual tours of nature reserves and observations of endangered species. This allows the public to more intuitively feel the beauty of ecology and the importance of ecological protection, thereby enhancing the effectiveness of dissemination.

3.3 Supports Assessing Ecological Culture Impact

Through data analysis and feedback mechanisms, disseminators can monitor the dissemination effects of content in real-time, understand the feedback and behavioral changes of the audience, and adjust communication strategies in a timely manner. For example, by analyzing the dwell time, interaction frequency, and behavioral paths of users on ecological culture platforms, disseminators can optimize the presentation of content and communication channels to ensure the efficient use of ecological culture dissemination resources. These technological advantages not only make up for the shortcomings of traditional communication methods but also inject new vitality into ecological culture dissemination, promoting its development towards a more efficient, precise, and influential direction.

4 Challenges in AI for Ecological Culture Dissemination

4.1 Technical Reliability and Accuracy Issues

AI is highly dependent on the accuracy of data and algorithms. However, data quality issues and algorithm biases may seriously affect the effectiveness of ecological culture dissemination. Ecological culture dissemination requires a large amount of data support, such as ecological environment monitoring data and public behavior data. If these data have quality issues, such as incompleteness, inaccuracy, or bias, it may lead to AI systems generating incorrect conclusions or recommendations.For example, in ecological data monitoring, sensor failures or inaccurate data collection may cause distorted monitoring data, which in turn affects the assessment of the ecological environment status and the accuracy of the dissemination content. In a nature reserve, an AI system was used to monitor the activity of wild animals. Due to sensor failures and data transmission errors, the system incorrectly judged the population and distribution of certain species, leading the reserve management department to take incorrect protection measures. This misjudgment not only wasted resources but also may have had a negative impact on the ecosystem. This case shows that data quality and algorithm reliability are key issues that must be resolved for the application of AI in ecological culture dissemination.

4.2 Privacy and Ethical Issues

During the process of ecological culture dissemination, AI systems need to collect and process a large amount of user data, including personal preferences, geographical locations, and behavioral habits. The collection and use of this data involve user privacy protection issues. If the data is leaked or misused, it will cause serious harm to users.

For example, a certain ecological culture platform, due to insufficient data protection measures, led to the leakage of user personal information, which triggered public concerns about data security and reduced user trust in the platform.In addition to privacy issues, the content generated by AI may also raise ethical controversies.

For example, some AI algorithms may generate misleading or inaccurate ecological information, which may even be maliciously used to spread false information. This phenomenon not only damages the public's trust in ecological culture dissemination but also may have a negative impact on ecological protection actions.

For example, a smart ecological culture application was found to have inaccurate information, leading users to misunderstand ecological protection measures and thereby affecting public participation enthusiasm.

4.3 Digital Divide and Dissemination Fairness Issues

The application of AI is highly dependent on the Internet and digital devices. However, there is still a significant digital divide worldwide. "The AI Ethics Guidelines" point out the principles of non-discrimination and fairness, that is, to achieve equal access and treatment through inclusive design. [8] However, people in remote areas, poor regions, and vulnerable groups may not be able to enjoy the convenience of ecological culture dissemination brought by artificial intelligence. Residents in some remote mountainous areas, due to the lack of network access and digital devices, cannot use artificial intelligence-based ecological culture platforms and applications. This results in these residents not being able to obtain timely and accurate ecological information, affecting the fairness of ecological culture dissemination. In remote mountainous areas, although local governments and environmental protection organizations actively promote the dissemination of ecological culture, due to weak network infrastructure and a lack of digital devices, residents cannot effectively use AI platforms to obtain ecological knowledge and participate in ecological protection activities. This digital divide not only limits the scope of ecological culture dissemination but also widens the gap in ecological awareness between regions.

4.4 Public Acceptance and Participation Issues

The complexity of AI may affect public acceptance and participation. Many users lack an understanding of AI and may even have misunderstandings and fears.

For example, some users may worry that AI will replace human jobs or pose a threat to personal privacy, thus being cautious about using AI platforms. This low acceptance due to the complexity of technology seriously affects the application effect of AI in ecological culture dissemination. For example, a smart ecological culture application received poor feedback during its promotion. Many users indicated that the application had a high technical threshold and was difficult to understand and use, eventually choosing to abandon it. This shows that the application of AI needs to fully consider the actual needs and operational capabilities of users, otherwise it will be difficult to gain widespread public support.

In summary, AI has great potential in the dissemination of ecological culture, but it also faces many challenges in terms of technical reliability, privacy and ethics, digital divide, and public acceptance. These challenges not only affect the effective application of AI but may also have a negative impact on the fairness and sustainability of ecological culture dissemination. Therefore, solving these challenges is the key to ensuring that AI plays a positive role in the dissemination of ecological culture.

5 Optimization Paths and Methods for AI

5.1 Enhancing Technical Reliability and Precision

Firstly, it is necessary to increase investment in the research and development of AI, encouraging research institutions and enterprises to conduct cutting-edge technology research, such as deep learning, natural language processing, and computer vision. By continuously optimizing algorithms, the ability of AI systems to process and analyze ecological data can be improved. For example, developing more advanced machine learning models that can more accurately identify subtle changes in ecosystems will provide more scientific and accurate information support for the dissemination of ecological culture.

Secondly, strengthening interdisciplinary research cooperation, combining the strengths of ecology, environmental science, computer science, and other disciplines to jointly tackle technical challenges. For example, ecologists can provide richer ecological knowledge and data for AI algorithms, helping them better understand and analyze ecological phenomena, while computer scientists can optimize algorithm performance and improve system efficiency and stability. This interdisciplinary cooperation can not only enhance the reliability of AI but also promote the depth and breadth of the content of ecological culture dissemination.

Furthermore, establishing a multi-source data fusion mechanism is essential. The dissemination of ecological culture involves a large amount of data, including ecological environment monitoring data, public behavior data, and socio-economic data. By integrating data from different sources, a more comprehensive understanding of the status of ecosystems and public needs can be achieved. For example, combining satellite remote sensing data, ground monitoring station data, and ecological information reported by the public can more accurately assess the health of ecosystems and provide richer background information for dissemination content.

Lastly, establishing an expert review mechanism is key to ensuring the accuracy and authority of content generated by artificial intelligence. The content of ecological culture dissemination often involves complex scientific knowledge and policy interpretation, which requires professional personnel to review and control. For example, ecologists can review ecological science articles generated by AI to ensure their scientific accuracy, while environmental policy experts can review policy interpretations in dissemination content to avoid misleading the public. Through the expert review mechanism, it is possible to effectively reduce misjudgments caused by data bias or algorithm errors in AI systems, thereby improving the quality and credibility of ecological culture dissemination.

5.2 Establishing a Comprehensive Privacy and Ethical Protection System

Firstly, it is essential to improve data privacy protection mechanisms. From a legal perspective, clear regulations on data collection, storage, use, and sharing must be established. Governments should enact strict privacy protection laws requiring ecological culture dissemination platforms to obtain explicit consent from users when collecting user data and to clearly inform users of the purposes and protective measures for the data. For example, the European Union's General Data Protection Regulation (GDPR) provides a strict legal framework for data privacy protection, which is worth learning from and referencing. Secondly, technical means are also crucial for ensuring data privacy. "A considerable portion of the data involved in AI contains personal privacy." [9] Ecological culture dissemination platforms should employ advanced encryption technologies to ensure the security of user data during transmission and storage. For example, end-to-end encryption technology can prevent data from being stolen or tampered with during transmission. Additionally, platforms should conduct regular security audits and vulnerability scans to identify and fix potential security risks in a timely manner.

Moreover, establishing strict access and management permissions for data is also very important. Only authorized personnel should be able to access user data, and all data access actions should be recorded and monitored. Through these measures, the abuse of user data by internal personnel can be effectively prevented, further enhancing the reliability of data privacy protection. Secondly, establishing a sound ethical review and regulation system for AI is essential. Ecological culture dissemination platforms should set up a dedicated ethics review committee composed of ecologists, ethicists, legal experts, and public representatives. This committee is responsible for conducting ethical reviews of content generated by AI to ensure that it complies with the principles of scientific accuracy and fairness. For example, for dissemination content involving the protection of endangered species, the ethics review committee should ensure that it does not mislead the public's understanding of the current status of species protection. At the same time, formulating ethical guidelines for AI is also an important measure to ensure the healthy development of ecological culture dissemination. These guidelines should clearly define the responsibilities and obligations of AI in the dissemination of ecological culture, requiring platforms to follow principles of transparency, fairness, and non-discrimination in content generation and dissemination. For example, guidelines should require platforms to avoid neglecting or overemphasizing certain ecological issues due to algorithmic bias when using AI algorithms. Additionally, strengthening ethical education and training in AI is an indispensable component. For technical personnel and content creators involved in ecological culture dissemination, regular ethical training should be conducted to enhance their awareness and sensitivity to ethical issues in artificial intelligence. Through these measures, the application of AI in ecological culture dissemination can not only meet technical standards but also comply with ethical and moral requirements.

5.3 Narrowing the Digital Divide to Promote Dissemination Fairness

On the one hand, strengthening the construction of digital infrastructure is crucial. "The adoption and application of intelligent technologies are constrained by economic, cultural, psychological, and other factors." [10] Governments should increase investment in network infrastructure construction in remote and poor areas to promote the broadband networks and mobile internet. Governments can collaborate with telecommunications operators, providing policy support and financial subsidies to encourage companies to lay fiber optic networks and build base stations in these areas, ensuring that residents have access to high-speed and stable internet. In addition to network infrastructure, the digital devices are also key to narrowing the digital divide. Governments can provide digital device support to remote and poor areas through various channels, such as educational poverty alleviation and cultural outreach programs.

For example, donating computers and tablet devices to schools, and establishing public libraries and digital learning centers to provide residents with free access to the internet and training services. Technological innovation is also an important means of narrowing the digital divide. For example, developing low-power, low-cost network access devices, such as solar-powered mobile devices and simple satellite communication terminals, can effectively reduce the cost for residents in remote areas to access the internet. At the same time, promoting the application of new technologies such as 5G and satellite internet can further expand network coverage and increase access speeds, providing stronger technical support for the dissemination of ecological culture.

On the other hand, developing communication tools suitable for different groups is essential. Improving digital infrastructure alone is insufficient; it is also necessary to develop communication tools tailored to different groups to ensure the fairness and effectiveness of ecological culture dissemination. For remote areas and vulnerable groups, developing simple-to-use, functionally targeted communication tools is crucial.

Additionally, developing accessible communication tools for the elderly and people with disabilities, such as large-font displays, voice announcements, and gesture controls, ensures that these groups can equally access ecological culture information. In multilingual regions, developing communication tools that support multiple languages is key to promoting dissemination fairness. For example, developing multilingual versions of ecological culture applications that offer options in minority languages and local dialects ensures that users with different language backgrounds can access ecological information without barriers. Through multilingual support, ecological culture can be more effectively disseminated, promoting the enhancement of ecological awareness among different regions and groups.

5.4 Inter-departmental Cooperation and Policy Support

Firstly, establishing a collaborative mechanism among governments, enterprises, and social organizations is essential. Governments can guide enterprises and social organizations to actively participate in the dissemination of ecological culture through policy-making, financial support, and platform-building. Enterprises can develop AI applications and platforms suitable for the dissemination of ecological culture through technological innovation. Social organizations play a bridging and linking role in inter-departmental cooperation. They can reach into communities, schools, and public groups to understand the public's needs and feedback regarding ecological culture, providing decision-making basis for governments and enterprises. At the same time, social organizations can also promote the implementation of ecological culture dissemination through organizing volunteer activities and conducting public welfare projects.

For example, social organizations can organize volunteer activities themed on ecological culture, guiding the public to participate in ecological protection practices and enhancing their sense of ecological responsibility.

Secondly, policy guidance and financial support are crucial. Governments should formulate clear policies to guide the application of AI in the dissemination of ecological culture. For example, establishing technical standards and regulations for the dissemination of ecological culture to ensure that the content generated by AI meets scientific and accurate requirements. At the same time, governments can guide enterprises and social organizations to develop and apply AI for ecological culture dissemination and ecological protection actions through policy incentives.

For example, by setting up demonstration projects for the dissemination of ecological culture, successful experiences and models can be promoted to encourage more entities to participate in ecological culture dissemination. In addition, governments can provide financial support for ecological culture dissemination projects through the establishment of special funds and financial subsidies.

For example, creating an "Innovation Fund for the Dissemination of Ecological Culture" to support research and implementation of AI applications in ecological culture dissemination. Governments can also cooperate with enterprises to establish a diversified funding mechanism. For example, through public-private partnership (PPP) models, social capital can be attracted to participate in ecological culture dissemination projects, jointly promoting the sustainable development of ecological culture dissemination.

6 Conclusion

This study has thoroughly explored the current opportunities and challenges of AI in the dissemination of ecological culture. The research indicates that artificial intelligence, with its powerful capabilities in data analysis, precise content delivery, and interactive experiences, offers unprecedented opportunities for the dissemination of ecological culture. It can effectively enhance the precision, coverage, and impact of dissemination efforts, thereby promoting the enhancement of public ecological awareness and the formation of green lifestyles. However, issues such as technical reliability, data privacy protection, the digital divide, and public acceptance pose significant challenges to the application of AI in this context.Through comprehensive analysis, this study proposes a series of optimization paths and methods, including enhancing technical reliability, improving privacy protection mechanisms, narrowing the digital divide, and strengthening inter-departmental cooperation. These measures aim to fully leverage the advantages of AI while overcoming its shortcomings, thereby providing stronger support for the dissemination of ecological culture.

References

1. Lu, R.: Ecological Culture Theory. Beijing Jiaotong University Press, Tsinghua University Press, October 2019. p. 205
2. Lu, R.: Ecological Culture Theory. Beijing Jiaotong University Press, Tsinghua University Press, October 2019. p. III
3. Chen, H., Tang, C.: Ecological Culture and Paradigm Transition. People's Publishing House, October 2013, p. 18
4. Thoreau, H.D.: Walden. Princeton University Press (1971)
5. Carson, R.L. Silent Spring. Penguin (2002)
6. Zhang, F.: Ethical reflections in the age of high technology. Philos. Trends **1**, 70–71 (2006)
7. Nagarajan, M., Felix, K.S.: Does artificial intelligence-based advertising improve the marketing and sales of a business? An outlook from e-commerce perspective. Int. J. Bus. Process Integr. Manage. **12**(2), 105–121 (2025)
8. Shen, Y., Wang, Q.: Ethical considerations of the application of artificial intelligence in education. Peking Univ. Educ. Rev. **4**, 18–34+184 (2019)
9. Xue, Q., Li, F.: Security risks of the educational application of artificial intelligence and counter measures. J. Distance Educ. **4**, 88–94 (2018)
10. Huang, R.: Artificial intelligence is accelerating educational transformation: real challenges and responses. Chin. Educ. Sci. J. **6**, 26–33 (2023)

Does Health Insurance Enhance the Subjective Well-Being of China's Rural-to-Urban Migrants?

Lei Yu[1(✉)], Wenqing Wang[1], and Xinlong Yang[2]

[1] Xi'an University of Technology, Xi'an, China
chsdcy@xaut.edu.cn

[2] Shenzhen Institute of Information Technology, Shenzhen, China

Abstract. This study examines whether health insurance enhances the subjective well-being (SWB) of China's rural-to-urban migrant workers. Despite their key contributions to economic development, these workers remain marginalized in the social security system. As a crucial component of social protection, health insurance may improve healthcare access and financial security, thus boosting well-being. Using data from the 2018 China Family Panel Studies (CFPS) and applying an ordered logit model, this paper explores the effects of health insurance participation. The findings suggest that both coverage and participation depth significantly improve migrant workers' SWB. Moreover, the effects vary across gender, education, and region. The study concludes with policy recommendations for government agencies, insurers, and migrant workers to enhance insurance effectiveness and support the well-being of this vulnerable population.

Keyword: Subjective Well-Being · Migrant Workers · Health Insurance

1 Introduction

Happiness is a fundamental human aspiration and a key indicator of economic and social development. Since the implementation of reform and opening-up policies, China has achieved remarkable progress in economic growth and political modernization, successfully transitioning into an upper-middle-income to high-income country and entering a phase of high-quality development. However, this prosperity has given rise to a "happiness paradox," in which gains in national income have not translated into proportional improvements in subjective well-being (SWB). In the context of socialism with Chinese characteristics in the new era, rising public demand for a better life has made enhancing SWB a central concern for governance at all administrative levels.

Among the groups most affected by this paradox are China's rural-to-urban migrants. Representing a significant portion of the labor force, they are often considered the backbone of China's urbanization and industrialization. According to the National Bureau of Statistics, there were approximately 297 million rural migrant workers in 2023. A report by the National Health Commission, titled "Safeguarding the Health Rights and Interests of Migrant Workers," underscores the urgency of addressing their health outcomes.

M. Luo and L.-J. Zhang (Eds.): SCC 2025, LNCS 16160, pp. 37–52, 2026.
https://doi.org/10.1007/978-3-032-06320-5_4

Between 1978 and 2015, migrant workers contributed 11.64% to non-agricultural output and 10.21% to total social output—figures that reflect their indispensable role in national development.

Despite these contributions, migrant workers often face structural barriers that hinder their well-being. Economic transitions, industrial restructuring, and exclusionary urban policies have led to their marginalization. Although China's social insurance system aims to promote social equity and economic security, many migrants struggle to access its benefits. Employers may under-enroll them to cut costs, while the migrants themselves often lack the financial resources or administrative knowledge to enroll independently. These obstacles undermine the welfare and risk-sharing functions that the social protection system is intended to fulfill.

In response, health insurance has emerged as a more accessible and targeted form of protection. With a lower participation threshold and a focus on basic medical needs, it complements the broader social insurance system and holds promise for improving migrant well-being. However, rigorous empirical evidence on the effectiveness of health insurance for migrant workers remains limited.

This study addresses this gap by examining whether and to what extent health insurance enhances the SWB of China's rural-to-urban migrants. It contributes to the literature in three key ways. First, while previous studies have examined the general population's well-being in relation to social insurance, few focus on the migrant workforce—a group with distinct vulnerabilities. Second, the study isolates the effect of health insurance, an underexplored element of China's social protection system. Third, it employs nationally representative micro-survey data and addresses endogeneity concerns through an instrumental variable (IV) approach, enhancing the credibility of causal inference.

2 Literature Review

2.1 Determinants of the SWB of Chinese Migrant Workers

Happiness is widely recognized as a core human aspiration and a key metric of socioeconomic progress. In China, it aligns closely with the national agenda of "common prosperity." Among the most vital yet vulnerable contributors to China's urbanization and economic development are rural-to-urban migrant workers. Despite their contributions, these individuals have historically been marginalized in urban systems and face barriers to full social integration. Recent years, however, have witnessed growing policy and academic attention toward improving their SWB (Yang & Zhang, 2016; Ye, 2011; Zhang, 2007; Chen & Xiong, 2020).

Existing literature in economics and psychology has explored the determinants of SWB among migrant workers, highlighting both economic and psychosocial dimensions. Early studies noted that although many migrant workers report happiness, their SWB is often lower than when they lived in rural areas(Zhang, 2007). Social support(Ye, 2011), marital status(Zhang, 2007), and family cohesion(Ye, 2011) appear to play more substantial roles than improvements in human capital alone. Several scholars have attempted to disentangle the causal mechanisms behind there observed discrepancies in SWB. For example, Zeng et al. (2016) noted that while labor migration may improve income, it can also reduce SWB due to emotional and social costs. Later works, such as Lu et al. (2017)

and Zhang et al. (2021), incorporated econometric techniques to address endogeneity, finding that income, perceived fairness, and social trust significantly impact SWB. However, many of these studies are case-specific and lack generalizability, while others do not account for endogeneity rigorously.

2.2 Studies on Insurance and SWB

Insurance is widely recognized as a tool to manage uncertainty and reduce vulnerability to financial shocks, thereby enhancing overall well-being. Theoretical perspectives from microeconomics suggest that insurance increases individual utility by stabilizing income and minimizing loss. Du (2016) and others have demonstrated positive associations between social insurance enrollment—especially health and pension coverage—and residents' SWB.

A growing body of literature distinguishes between the effects of social and commercial insurance (Liu, 2015; Cao et al., 2020). Studies have shown that participation in social insurance programs, such as health or pension schemes, significantly improves SWB, particularly among rural, low-income, and older populations (Liu, 2015; Fang & Sakellariou, 2016). Huang and Guo (2018) provide empirical support for this urban–rural gap using CGSS data, showing stronger insurance effects on well-being in rural areas. Yet, concerns persist regarding inefficiencies in programs like the New Rural Cooperative Medical System (NRCMS), where low reimbursement rates and administrative challenges limit their effectiveness. Huo and Chen (2017) further attribute the limited happiness gains under NRCMS to bureaucratic procedures and low perceived returns on participation. Some studies, like those by Chen and Xiong (2020), have used instrumental variable strategies to demonstrate causal impacts, especially among vulnerable elderly groups. However, findings across regions and income groups remain inconsistent (Zhang & Tan, 2018). In contrast, research on commercial insurance—although limited in the Chinese context—suggests a positive correlation with SWB, especially for higher-income households and rural participants (Cao et al., 2020). Sang (2019) provides micro-level survey evidence that household happiness strongly predicts commercial insurance participation, suggesting a feedback between satisfaction and market-based choices.

Despite these insights, two important research gaps persist. First, existing studies focus rarely focus on migrant workers as a structurally vulnerable subgroup. Second, the psychological pathways through which insurance affects well-being remain under-explored. To address these gaps, this study utilizes CFPS 2018 data and employs ordered logit(OLOGIT) and OLS regression, supplemented with instrumental variable techniques, to identify the causal effect of health insurance participation on the well-being of migrant workers. By doing so, it offers both empirical and policy contributions to China's evolving health security system.

2.3 Theoretical Framework and Hypotheses

To empirically examine these theoretical propositions, this study focuses on two core constructs: health insurance coverage (whether an individual is insured) and depth of participation (measured by the number or comprehensiveness of insurance policies held). Health insurance may enhance well-being not only by improving access to medical care, but also by reducing financial anxiety and enhancing perceived security and control over future health risks. Based on the above theoretical framework, we propose the following hypotheses:

H1: Health insurance coverage has a positive effect on the SWB of migrant workers.
H2: The depth of health insurance participation positively influences the SWB of migrant workers.
H3: The effect of health insurance on SWB varies by gender, education level, and region, reflecting heterogeneity arising from social comparison and stratification mechanisms.

By testing these hypotheses, this study offers a theoretically grounded and policy-relevant analysis of how health insurance affects the well-being of rural-to-urban migrants—one of China's most socioeconomically vulnerable groups—within the context of an evolving social security system.

3 Methodology

3.1 Data and Variables

This study uses data from the 2018 China Family Panel Studies (CFPS), a nationally representative longitudinal survey covering 25 provinces and conducted by Peking University. It includes over 16,000 households with detailed information on demographics, economic conditions, health status, insurance, and SWB. The CFPS provides a solid empirical basis for analyzing how health insurance affects rural-to-urban migrant workers' well-being.

The two key explanatory variables are health insurance coverage and depth of participation. Insurance coverage is measured using two CFPS questions: (1) employer-provided or self-purchased insurance, and (2) current health insurance types. A binary variable is coded as 1 if respondents selected "2" in the first question and reported any valid option in the second; otherwise, it is 0. The depth of participation is proxied by annual household expenditure on commercial health insurance, with its logarithmic value used to reduce skewness.

SWB is assessed through three self-reported variables: life satisfaction, subjective social status, and perceived income level—each based on five-point Likert scales. These indicators reflect psychological, social, and economic dimensions of well-being and are treated as ordinal variables in the analysis. While self-reported measures capture individuals' perceptions, they may also be influenced by temporary emotions or response styles. Future studies could complement subjective assessments with objective indicators to validate the findings.

To reduce confounding bias, control variables include individual, household, and regional factors: age, gender, marital status, education, party membership, health status, assets, income, consumption, and regional location (Eastern, Central, Western).

However, the CFPS data lack granularity in distinguishing insurance types or measuring service quality, which may bias individuals' perceived well-being. Moreover, as cross-sectional data, they limit the ability to infer causality or assess long-term dynamics. Future research should incorporate panel data to address these limitations.

3.2 Model Specification

The three dependent variables—life satisfaction, perceived social status, and subjective income level—are measured on five-point ordinal scales ranging from 1 ("very dissatisfied/low") to 5 ("very satisfied/high"). Given their ordered nature, this study employs an OLOGIT model to examine the relationship between health insurance and subjective well-being. The OLOGIT model assumes that the observed ordinal outcome is driven by an underlying continuous latent variable representing SWB. The empirical model is specified as follows:

$$\text{Happy}_i = \alpha + \beta\,\text{Insurance}_i + \lambda\,\text{CV}_i + \varepsilon_i \tag{1}$$

where:

- Happy_i denotes the SWB of individual i, proxied by one of three measures: life satisfaction, subjective social status, or perceived income level;
- Insurance_i represents the main independent variable of interest, which includes health insurance coverage and insurance expenditure (log-transformed);
- CV_i is a vector of control variables, including age, gender, marital status, education level, party membership, self-rated health, household income, household assets, household expenditures, and regional dummies;
- α is the intercept term;
- β and λ are the vectors of coefficients to be estimated;
- ε_i is the error term, assumed to follow a logistic distribution.

This framework estimates the probability that an individual's latent well-being level lies between thresholds corresponding to the observed categorical outcomes (from 1 to 5). This approach is well-suited to modeling ordinal outcomes and provides meaningful insights into how health insurance participation influences SWB among migrant workers.

4 Estimation Results

4.1 Descriptive Statistics

Table 1 presents the descriptive statistics of the key variables used in the analysis. The mean value of life satisfaction among rural-to-urban migrant workers is 3.974, with a standard deviation of 0.996, indicating that, on average, most respondents are relatively satisfied with their lives. The average score for subjective social status is 3.120, suggesting that most migrant workers perceive themselves as occupying a middle-tier position in the social hierarchy. The mean value for subjective income level is 2.918, with a standard deviation of 1.094, implying that migrant workers tend to view their income as average relative to others in their community. Regarding health insurance participation, approximately 91.1% of respondents report being covered by at least one form of health insurance, as indicated by the binary variable with a mean of 0.911. The log-transformed commercial insurance expenditure variable has a mean of 2.439 and a standard deviation of 3.719, reflecting that while many migrant workers invest in commercial insurance, the actual amount spent varies widely and is generally modest.

Demographic statistics reveal that the average age of the sample is 44.2 years, and 49.9% of the respondents are male. The majority of participants are married, as indicated by a mean value of 2.037 for the marital status variable (which is categorical). Educational attainment is relatively low, with a mean value of 0.990 (on a scale from 0 to 3), suggesting that most respondents have completed only primary to high school education. Only 5% of the respondents are members of the Communist Party, indicating limited political affiliation among this group. The average self-rated health status is 2.959, suggesting that most migrant workers perceive their health as moderately good. In terms of household economic indicators, the mean values for household property, income, and expenditure are 11.98, 10.61, and 10.18, respectively, all measured on log-transformed scales. These values indicate that the sample has relatively stable economic conditions, although with some variation. Finally, the regional distribution of the sample, as represented by the variable "Area" (mean = 2.299), shows that migrant workers are unevenly distributed across China's four regions. Specifically, 26.67% of the sample is from the eastern region, 25.82% from the central region, 38.61% from the western region, and 8.95% from the northeastern region.

Table 1. Descriptive Statistics of Variables.

Variables	Obs.	Mean	Std. Dev.	Min	Max
Satisfaction	11548	3.974	0.996	1	5
Identity	11510	3.120	1.112	1	5
Income-level	10788	2.918	1.094	1	5
Insurance	11679	0.911	0.284	0	1
Ins-expenditure	11452	2.439	3.719	0	11.16
Age	11679	44.20	15.88	16	95
Gender	11679	0.499	0.500	0	1
Marriage	11679	2.037	0.807	1	5
Education	6744	0.909	0.517	0	3
Party	11679	0.050	0.218	0	1
Health	11524	2.959	1.253	1	5
Property	11602	11.98	1.451	0	17.51
Income	11370	10.61	0.972	0	13.46
Expenditure	11356	10.18	0.951	0	14.22
Area	11678	2.299	0.960	1	4

4.2 The Impact of Health Insurance on Migrant Workers' SWB

Table 2 reports the results from the OLOGIT regressions examining the effect of health insurance coverage on three dimensions of SWB among rural-to-urban migrant workers in China. In Model 1, the coefficient for health insurance is 0.200, indicating that migrant workers who are enrolled in health insurance report significantly higher levels of life satisfaction compared to those without coverage. This suggests a 20.0% increase in the likelihood of reporting higher satisfaction, confirming the positive association at the 5% level of statistical significance. In Model 2, health insurance coverage also exhibits a significant positive effect on subjective social status, with a coefficient of 0.278, corresponding to a marginal effect of 27.8%. This implies that insured individuals are substantially more likely to perceive themselves as having a higher social position. Model 3 shows that health insurance has a positive and significant effect on subjective income perception, with a coefficient of 0.183, translating to a marginal effect of 18.3%. Together, the findings from all three models provide robust empirical support for Hypothesis 1, which posits that health insurance coverage significantly enhances the SWB of Chinese migrant workers.

With regard to the control variables, age is positively and significantly associated with SWB across all models (coefficients range from 0.017 to 0.026), suggesting a life-cycle pattern in happiness. Younger respondents may experience lower well-being due to education and employment pressures, while older individuals report higher well-being owing to greater life stability and reduced expectations. Gender shows a consistent negative and statistically significant effect, with males reporting lower levels of well-being than females. This pattern aligns with prior findings on gender differences in emotional resilience and life satisfaction. Marital status has a negative but statistically insignificant effect. Education level is significantly negatively associated with well-being in all three models (e.g., −0.324 in Model 1), which may reflect higher expectations and goal stress among more educated individuals. Political affiliation (Party membership) shows mixed effects: a positive association with life satisfaction (0.229, not significant), but negative or insignificant effects on social status and income perception. These results suggest that while Party affiliation may offer some intangible benefits, it does not uniformly enhance all aspects of SWB. Health status has a strong and consistently significant positive effect on well-being across all models, further reinforcing the foundational role of health in determining happiness.

At the household level, both total property and income are positively associated with SWB, whereas expenditure is negatively associated. These results support the conventional view that greater wealth and lower spending burdens contribute to higher life satisfaction.

Finally, regional differences are evident. Migrant workers in the Northeast report the highest levels of SWB, followed by those in the West, Central, and East. The Eastern region, despite being economically developed, shows the lowest levels of well-being, likely due to high housing costs, competitive labor markets, and elevated living pressures.

Table 2. Ordered Logit Regression Results: Health Insurance and SWB of Migrant Workers

VARIABLES	(1)	(2)	(3)
	Satisfaction	Identity	Income-level
Insurance	0.200**	0.278***	0.183**
	(0.080)	(0.082)	(0.088)

(continued)

Table 2. (*continued*)

VARIABLES	(1)	(2)	(3)
	Satisfaction	Identity	Income-level
Age	0.026***	0.029***	0.017***
	(0.003)	(0.002)	(0.003)
Gender	−0.155***	−0.169***	−0.162***
	(0.047)	(0.047)	(0.050)
Marriage	−0.047	−0.047	−0.062
	(0.041)	(0.041)	(0.043)
Education	−0.324***	−0.232***	−0.210***
	(0.054)	(0.054)	(0.056)
Party	−0.071	0.250**	0.134
	(0.122)	(0.119)	(0.124)
Health	−0.414***	−0.284***	−0.302***
	(0.022)	(0.022)	(0.023)
Property	−0.028*	0.020	0.037**
	(0.017)	(0.017)	(0.018)
Income	0.075**	0.042	0.165***
	(0.032)	(0.032)	(0.035)
Expenditure	−0.021	−0.055*	−0.060*
	(0.029)	(0.029)	(0.031)
Area	0.005	0.106***	0.091***
	(0.025)	(0.025)	(0.026)
Observations	6,351	6,333	5,753
R-squared	0.032	0.024	0.018

Note: Standard deviations are in parentheses and ***, **, and * indicate significant at the 1%, 5%, and 10% levels, respectively. The marginal effects estimated by the Probit model are reported in the table. The same as below

4.3 The Impact of Health Insurance Participation Depth on the SWB of Migrant Workers

Table 3 presents the results of the regression analysis examining the effect of the depth of health insurance participation—measured by log-transformed insurance expenditure—on the SWB of rural-to-urban migrant workers. In Model 1, the coefficient on insurance expenditure is 0.0168, indicating that a higher level of investment in health insurance is significantly associated with greater life satisfaction. Specifically, a one-unit increase in log health insurance expenditure is associated with a 1.68% increase in life satisfaction.

This result is statistically significant at the 1% level. Model 2 shows that the depth of health insurance participation also has a significant positive effect on subjective social status, with a marginal effect of 1.74%. This suggests that increased financial investment in health insurance improves not only perceived well-being but also one's sense of social position. In Model 3, the coefficient on insurance expenditure is 0.001, which is positive but not statistically significant, indicating a weaker association between the depth of health insurance participation and perceived income level. Taken together, the findings from Models 1 to 3 provide empirical support for Hypothesis 2, which posits that greater depth of participation in health insurance contributes to higher levels of SWB among Chinese migrant workers.

As for control variables, age consistently exhibits a positive and statistically significant association with SWB across all models, with marginal effects of 2.63%, 3.06%, and 1.78%, respectively. This reflects a life-cycle pattern: younger individuals experience greater academic and career-related stress; middle-aged individuals face family and financial pressures; while older individuals, benefitting from stability and lower expectations, report higher well-being. Gender shows a significant negative effect on well-being, with male migrant workers being 15.0% to 17.2% less likely to report high well-being than females. This may reflect differences in emotional expression, social support, or work-related stress. Marital status has a negative but statistically insignificant effect in all models. Educational attainment is negatively and significantly associated with well-being, consistent with the notion that higher expectations among more educated individuals may lead to greater dissatisfaction when aspirations are unmet. Political affiliation (i.e., Party membership) has a positive and significant effect on life satisfaction, but not on subjective identity or income perception. Health status shows a strong and significant positive effect on all dimensions of SWB. A one-unit increase in self-rated health is associated with 4.12%, 2.85%, and 3.03% increases in life satisfaction, class identity, and income perception, respectively—highlighting health as a fundamental foundation of well-being.

At the household level, both property and income are positively correlated with SWB, while expenditure has a negative effect, suggesting that material security contributes to life satisfaction, while financial burdens reduce it.

Finally, there are clear regional disparities. Consistent across models, migrant workers in the Northeast report the highest levels of SWB, followed by those in the Western, Central, and Eastern regions. The Eastern region, despite its economic advancement, is associated with lower well-being, likely due to higher living costs, housing prices, and work-related stress.

Table 3. Ordered Logit Regression Results: Impact of Health Insurance Participation Depth on the SWB of Migrant Workers

VARIABLES	(1)	(2)	(3)
	Satisfaction	Identity	Income-level
Ins-expenditure	0.0168***	0.0174***	0.0012
	(0.0064)	(0.0064)	(0.0068)

(continued)

Table 3. (*continued*)

VARIABLES	(1)	(2)	(3)
	Satisfaction	Identity	Income-level
Age	0.0263***	0.0306***	0.0177***
	(0.0025)	(0.0025)	(0.0027)
Gender	−0.1500***	−0.1720***	−0.1670***
	(0.0473)	(0.0475)	(0.0500)
Marriage	−0.0452	−0.0511	−0.0641
	(0.0416)	(0.0412)	(0.0432)
Education	−0.3330***	−0.222***	−0.2150***
	(0.0541)	(0.0544)	(0.0563)
Party	−0.0693	0.2490**	0.1370
	(0.1230)	(0.1190)	(0.1250)
Health	−0.412***	−0.2850***	−0.3030***
	(0.0226)	(0.0221)	(0.0230)
Property	−0.0343**	0.0166	0.0378**
	(0.0173)	(0.0178)	(0.0183)
Income	0.0679**	0.0294	0.1710***
	(0.0326)	(0.0324)	(0.0357)
Expenditure	−0.0256	−0.0559*	−0.0575*
	(0.0293)	(0.0295)	(0.0310)
Area	0.0041	0.1050***	0.0879***
	(0.0255)	(0.0255)	(0.0267)
Observations	6,260	6,242	5,665
R-squared	0.0320	0.0240	0.0170

4.4 Robustness Test: Addressing Endogeneity via Instrumental Variable Estimation

The relationship between health insurance participation and the SWB of migrant workers may suffer from endogeneity due to omitted variable bias, measurement error, or reverse causality. On one hand, SWB may be influenced by unobserved factors not fully accounted for in the baseline model. On the other hand, happier individuals may be more inclined to participate in health insurance plans, introducing bidirectional causality between the independent and dependent variables.

To address this concern, the study employs a two-stage least squares (2SLS) instrumental variable (IV) approach. Following Chen and Fan (2010) and Fan et al. (2019), a valid instrumental variable must be strongly correlated with the endogenous explanatory variable (health insurance participation), but uncorrelated with the error term in the outcome equation. Based on the approach of Hu and Zhu (2023), this study selects the provincial-level health insurance participation rate as the instrumental variable.

Specifically, this variable is constructed from the CFPS data by calculating the proportion of individuals covered by health insurance within each province-level group of rural migrant workers. This aggregated coverage rate serves as an external instrument, as it is plausibly correlated with an individual's likelihood of insurance participation but not directly with their SWB.

The estimation results from the IV approach are presented in Table 4. Model (1) reports the first-stage regression, showing that the instrumental variable has a significant and positive association with individual health insurance participation. The associated F-statistic is 24.7, well above the conventional threshold of 10, suggesting that the instrument is sufficiently strong and not weak.

Models (2) to (4) present the second-stage regressions, where the predicted value of health insurance participation is used to estimate its effect on the three dependent variables. The results show that insurance participation significantly enhances all aspects of SWB: it increases life satisfaction (coefficient = 0.844), has an even stronger effect on subjective social status (coefficient = 1.658), and positively influences subjective income perception (coefficient = 0.807), all statistically significant.

These findings reaffirm the robustness of the baseline results: even after accounting for potential endogeneity, health insurance participation exerts a statistically significant and positive effect on various dimensions of SWB among migrant workers.

Other covariates generally show patterns consistent with the baseline models. Age is positively associated with well-being; education exhibits a negative effect; health and income show strong positive associations; and expenditure has a negative relationship. While political affiliation (Party membership) remains positively associated with insurance participation, its effects on well-being outcomes are mixed.

In conclusion, the use of the instrumental variable approach strengthens the credibility of the study's findings. After correcting for endogeneity, the core result still holds: health insurance participation plays a significant role in enhancing the SWB of Chinese rural-to-urban migrant workers.

Table 4. Two-Stage Least Squares Regression Results

VARIABLES	(1) Insurance	(2) Satisfaction	(3) Identity	(4) Income-level
IV	0.012***			
	(12.090)			
Insurance		0.844***	1.658***	0.807**
		(3.040)	(4.980)	(2.570)
Age	0.002***	0.011***	0.013***	0.009***
	(4.990)	(7.900)	(8.220)	(5.880)
Marriage	0.027***	−0.051**	−0.062**	−0.049**
	(4.330)	(−2.300)	(−2.390)	(−1.990)

(*continued*)

Table 4. (*continued*)

VARIABLES	(1) Insurance	(2) Satisfaction	(3) Identity	(4) Income-level
Education	0.023***	−0.147***	−0.159***	−0.134***
	(2.740)	(−5.090)	(−4.720)	(−4.200)
Party	0.048**	−0.081	0.045	0.034
	(2.510)	(−1.240)	(0.600)	(0.470)
Health	0.002	−0.197***	−0.157***	−0.162***
	(0.520)	(−17.760)	(−12.160)	(−13.040)
Property	−0.001	−0.010	0.014	0.021**
	(−0.190)	(−1.070)	(1.310)	(2.050)
Income	0.016***	0.034**	0.002	0.075***
	(3.260)	(1.970)	(0.070)	(3.720)
Expenditure	0.009**	−0.012	−0.044**	−0.039**
	(1.990)	(−0.760)	(−2.390)	(−2.200)
Area	0.002	0.010	0.054***	0.051***
	(0.500)	(0.720)	(3.360)	(3.380)
Constant	−0.556***	3.440***	1.887***	1.746***
	(−5.190)	(14.210)	(6.530)	(6.240)
Observations	6,351	6,351	6,333	5,753
R-squared	0.041	0.047	0.025	0.030

4.5 Heterogeneity Analysis

While the baseline regressions demonstrate that health insurance coverage and the depth of participation significantly enhance the SWB of rural-to-urban migrant workers, these effects may vary across subgroups due to differences in socioeconomic characteristics. To examine this, we conducted subgroup analyses based on educational attainment and regional location using OLOGIT models. While the main regression models examine three dimensions of SWB—life satisfaction, perceived social status, and subjective income level—the heterogeneity analysis focuses exclusively on life satisfaction as the dependent variable. This choice reflects both its conceptual centrality and empirical robustness, and allows for a more concise subgroup comparison. Control variables—such as age, gender, income, marital status, and employment status—are included in all regressions but omitted from discussion for brevity, as their marginal effects remain largely consistent across subgroups.

4.5.1 Educational Heterogeneity

As shown in Table 5, the positive effect of health insurance is concentrated among migrant workers with primary or secondary education. For this group, the coefficient for insurance coverage is 0.217, while the coefficient for insurance expenditure is 0.014, indicating both dimensions significantly improve SWB. In contrast, neither effect is statistically significant among respondents with no formal education or with tertiary qualifications.

This pattern suggests that moderately educated individuals—who typically possess basic financial literacy and a greater openness to formal protection mechanisms—derive the greatest psychological benefits from insurance. Conversely, those without schooling may lack awareness of how insurance functions, while more highly educated individuals may hold higher expectations or seek alternative private coverage, reducing the marginal utility of public insurance.

Table 5. Heterogeneous Effects of Health Insurance on SWB by Education

VARIABLES	(1) No Formal Education	(2) Primary to High School	(3) College and Above
Insurance	0.116	0.217**	0.050
	(0.222)	(0.091)	(0.292)
Ins-expenditure	0.018	0.014*	0.018
	(0.018)	(0.007)	(0.021)
Age	0.025***	0.028***	−0.003
	(0.005)	(0.003)	(0.021)
Gender	−0.150	−0.125**	−0.406**
	(0.120)	(0.055)	(0.160)
Marriage	−0.045	−0.101*	0.334*
	(0.072)	(0.054)	(0.177)
party	−0.282	−0.082	−0.007
	(0.344)	(0.159)	(0.260)
Health	−0.236***	−0.484***	−0.363***
	(0.045)	(0.028)	(0.084)
Property	−0.148***	−0.014	−0.032
	(0.045)	(0.021)	(0.052)
Income	0.174*	0.048	0.121
	(0.090)	(0.036)	(0.141)
Expenditure	−0.187**	−0.005	0.093
	(0.076)	(0.034)	(0.114)
Area	0.119*	−0.013	−0.053

(*continued*)

Table 5. (*continued*)

VARIABLES	(1) No Formal Education	(2) Primary to High School	(3) College and Above
	(0.070)	(0.029)	(0.086)
Observations	1,133	4,565	562
R-squared	0.025	0.030	0.026

4.5.2 Regional Heterogeneity

Regional analysis (Table 6) reveals that the eastern region exhibits the strongest and most statistically significant association between health insurance and well-being. The coefficient for insurance coverage in the east is 0.386, and for insurance expenditure, 0.0468, indicating that both access and depth of participation yield clear psychological benefits in economically developed areas. In contrast, the effects in central and western regions are smaller and largely insignificant. Notably, the coefficient in the northeastern region is negative, albeit statistically insignificant, suggesting potential dissatisfaction or inefficiency in policy implementation there.

Table 6. Heterogeneous Effects of Health Insurance on SWB by Region

VARIABLES	(1) Eastern Region	(2) Central Region	(3) Western Region	(4) Northeastern Region
Insurance	0.386**	0.257	0.116	−0.255
	(0.150)	(0.162)	(0.139)	(0.232)
Ins-expenditure	0.047***	0.006	−0.004	0.037
	(0.012)	(0.012)	(0.011)	(0.024)
Age	0.021***	0.018***	0.027***	0.049***
	(0.005)	(0.005)	(0.004)	(0.009)
Gender	−0.065	−0.217**	−0.095	−0.292*
	(0.094)	(0.094)	(0.075)	(0.168)
Marriage	0.024	0.083	−0.161***	−0.112
	(0.091)	(0.090)	(0.061)	(0.134)
Education	−0.165	−0.586***	−0.424***	0.094
	(0.112)	(0.115)	(0.082)	(0.227)
party	−0.022	0.058	−0.305	0.720
	(0.236)	(0.265)	(0.187)	(0.473)
Health	−0.532***	−0.471***	−0.292***	−0.495***
	(0.046)	(0.045)	(0.035)	(0.077)

(*continued*)

Table 6. (*continued*)

VARIABLES	(1) Eastern Region	(2) Central Region	(3) Western Region	(4) Northeastern Region
Property	−0.029	−0.068*	−0.016	−0.060
	(0.032)	(0.036)	(0.027)	(0.081)
Income	0.105*	0.042	0.064	−0.027
	(0.061)	(0.076)	(0.052)	(0.091)
Expenditure	−0.115**	0.124*	−0.054	0.035
	(0.055)	(0.068)	(0.046)	(0.090)
Observations	1,584	1,589	2,568	519
R-squared	0.044	0.044	0.027	0.057

5 Conclusions and Policy Implications

This paper empirically examines the impact of health insurance on the SWB of rural-to-urban migrant workers in China, using micro-level data from the CFPS. The findings contribute to the literature on migrant well-being and offer evidence for policy design. Two key insights emerge. First, both coverage and participation depth significantly improve well-being across dimensions such as life satisfaction, perceived social status, and subjective income. Second, the effects are heterogeneous: the benefits are more pronounced among male migrants, those with primary or secondary education, and residents in the eastern region. These results highlight the need for tailored policies to address the diverse needs within the migrant workforce.

One limitation of this study is that it does not account for employment conditions, which may also influence migrant workers' well-being. Prior research (Singh & Singh, 2019) has shown that job formality significantly affects job satisfaction, suggesting that future studies should consider the interplay between labor market status and social security coverage.

Based on these findings, several policy recommendations are proposed. First, the government should improve the regulatory framework for health insurance and offer financial support, such as tax incentives, to encourage broader participation. Second, insurance providers should enhance the experience of the insured by strengthening collaboration between insurance departments, improving protection mechanisms, aligning services with the needs of migrant workers, and raising the quality and accessibility of their products (Daneshgar et al., 2006). In addition, both public institutions and private insurers should promote insurance awareness through targeted education campaigns to improve health insurance literacy. Strengthening the coverage, quality, and visibility of health insurance can not only improve individual well-being but also promote social equity, public trust, and long-term stability in China's rapidly urbanizing society.

References

Cao, Z., Ye, X., Wu, F.: The impact of residents' happiness on family commercial insurance: a transmission mechanism test based on the heterogeneity perspective. J. Jiangxi Univ. Finance Econ. **02**, 62–75 (2020)

Chen, L., Xiong, M.: The happiness effect of basic medical insurance system. Soc. Secur. Res. **05**, 51–62 (2020)

Chen, Y., Fan, X.: A review of research on endogeneity issues in quantitative sociological analyses to measure the causal effects of social interactions. Society **30**(04), 91–117 (2010)

Chu, L., Xing, Z.: Basic medical insurance and residents' sense of well-being: an empirical analysis based on CGSS2012 and CGSS2017 survey data. Shandong Soc. Sci. **10**, 86–94 (2020)

Daneshgar, F., Bunker, D., Mawson Lee, K.: Identifying opportunities for strengthening cooperation in the Australian health insurance sector. Int. J. Bus. Process. Integr. Manag. **1**(4), 277–286 (2006)

Du, X.: Can purchasing insurance improve the happiness of urban residents? Analysis based on Chinese household income survey data. South. Finan. **04**, 73–80 (2016)

Fang, Z., Sakellariou, C.: Social insurance, income and subjective well-being of rural migrants in China: an application of unconditional quantile regression. J. Happiness Stud. **17**, 1635–1657 (2016)

Fan, H., Liu, S., Chen, L.: Whether commercial health insurance promotes residents' health: an empirical study based on microdata. Insur. Res. **03**, 116–127 (2019)

Huang, X., Guo, S.: Research on the implicit welfare valuation and mechanism of health insurance under the perspective of urban-rural differences: an empirical analysis based on CGSS subjective well-being data. J. Huazhong Agric. Univ. (Soc. Sci. Ed.) (06), 93–103+156 (2018)

Huo, L., Chen, Y.: "New Rural Cooperative Programme": have farmers gained a sense of happiness? J. Shanghai Univ. Finan. Econ. **19**(02), 38–49 (2017)

Hu, H., Zhu, T.: Commercial insurance for common wealth enhancement: mechanisms and effects. Insur. Res. **11**, 3–20 (2023)

Liu, Y.: Empirical study on the happiness effect of social security system: based on the perspective of medical insurance and pension insurance. Res. Bus. Econ. **06**, 92–94 (2015)

Lu, H., Yang, L., Li, B.: Employment quality, social cognition and rural migrant workers' happiness. China Rural Obs. **03**, 57–71 (2017)

Sang, L.: Research on the impact of social health insurance on residents' happiness and internal mechanism. Soc. Secur. Res. **06**, 31–45 (2018)

Sang, L.: Residents' happiness, subjective attitudes and commercial insurance market participation: a study based on Chinese household finance survey data. Econ. Manage. **33**(02), 45–53 (2019)

Singh, J., Singh, H.: Comparison of job satisfaction between staff and labor in steel industry of Northern India–an empirical investigation. Int. J. Bus. Process. Integr. Manag. **9**(4), 316–335 (2019)

Yang, Y., Zhang, S.: Sense of income inequality, social insurance and national happiness in China. Fin. Res. **08**, 34–50 (2016)

Ye, P.: An empirical analysis of migrant workers' subjective well-being in urban life. Youth Res. (03), 39–47+95 (2011)

Zeng, D., Hong, Y.: The impact of labor migration on the well-being of migrant workers in the context of urbanization. J. Nanjing Agric. Univ. (Soc. Sci. Ed.) **16**(06), 49–60+153–154 (2016)

Zhang, J., Chen, Z., Ding, S.: A study of employment quality, social trust and subjective well-being of migrant workers. J. Huazhong Agric. Univ. (Soc. Sci. Ed.) (02), 128–137+181–182 (2021)

Zhang, X.: Analysis of subjective happiness and its influencing factors of migrant workers: taking 512 migrant workers in Wuhan as an example. Soc. Work **05**, 48–51 (2007)

Zhang, Z., Tan, Y.: Social insurance and national happiness in China. Res. Fin. Econ. **33**(03), 116–128 (2018)

Research on the Evaluation of Teachers' Ability in Higher Vocational Colleges Under the Background of Digital Transformation: Theoretical Framework and System Design

Li Xu[1(✉)], Xinlong Yang[2], and Rong Ye[1]

[1] Tourism College of Zhejiang, Zhejiang, Hangzhou 311231, China
xuli@tourzj.edu.cn

[2] Shenzhen Institute of Information Technology, Shenzhen 518172, China

Abstract. The development of a practical, comprehensive, scientific, and rational evaluation index system for teachers' ability is critically important for enhancing the quality and capabilities of educators in higher vocational colleges, as well as for fostering the high-quality development of higher vocational education. Therefore, this study first examined the suitability of the CIPP model for evaluating teachers' ability and constructed a theoretical framework for such evaluations. This framework includes four dimensions: context evaluation, input evaluation, process evaluation, and product evaluation. Furthermore, the Delphi-AHP method was used to develop an evaluative index system that assesses teachers' ability. This system comprises four primary indexes (fundamental ability, conditional ability, practical ability, and developmental ability), twenty secondary indexes, and fifty-six tertiary indexes. The aim is to provide a theoretical foundation for establishing a robust teachers' ability evaluation system in higher vocational colleges.

Keywords: Teachers' ability · Evaluation system · CIPP model · Higher vocational colleges

1 Introduction

The overall quality of the teaching staff plays a decisive role in the quality of talent cultivation in higher vocational education, and their overall ability is the key to determining the quality of talent cultivation.

In recent years, the government has issued a series of policy documents strengthen the construction of college teachers. These policies emphasize the importance of ideological, political, and moral development, advocate for a quality-oriented approach, propose an evaluation system that prioritizes academic contributions, social impact, and support for talent cultivation, so as to comprehensively improve both the quality and competence of educators [1]. Especially in the context of digital transformation, it is imperative for educators to possess not only conventional teaching and research aptitudes but also competencies in the utilization of digital teaching instruments, proficiency

M. Luo and L.-J. Zhang (Eds.): SCC 2025, LNCS 16160, pp. 53–68, 2026.
https://doi.org/10.1007/978-3-032-06320-5_5

in data analysis, and the capacity to guide students in adapting to prospective digital work environments. This has emerged as a new dimension for assessing teachers' professional quality. As vocational education gains prominence, establishing a robust evaluation system for teachers' ability has become essential for effective modern vocational education and is critical for fostering professional growth among educators. Consequently, the construction of an evaluation system for teachers' ability in higher vocational colleges that align with the demands of digital transformation and educational reform is an inevitable necessity.

Higher vocational education, representing a significant segment of the higher education landscape, and holds an equivalent status to general higher education and serves as a cornerstone of the modern vocational educational system [2]. In the early 1980s, higher vocational education has experienced substantial growth in China. After decades marked by rapid advancement and ongoing enhancement efforts, it has evolved into one of the most sought-after forms of higher learning, accounting for over half of all enrolments annually across various institutions [3]. Therefore, elevating the overall quality of teaching staff within higher vocational colleges is crucial for advancing reform initiatives and fostering sustainable development in this sector. However, there are many prominent problems in the construction of the teaching staff in higher vocational colleges that need to be urgently solved, which are mainly reflected in the following aspects: firstly, the construction mechanism of teachers' team is not optimal, and the standardization needs to be improved; secondly, the absence of scientific and unified standards for teachers' abilities, coupled with an inadequate evaluation system, is conspicuous; thirdly, the direction and goal of the construction of teaching staff are not sufficiently clear, and lack of systematic planning and long-term layout [1, 3]. Additionally, the multifaceted nature of teachers' responsibilities, encompassing complex teaching activities, scientific research, social services, and other dimensions, results in disparate requirements for teachers' ability across different disciplines and positions. This heterogeneity complicates the establishment of unified evaluation criteria for teachers' ability [3]. In view of this, in order to promote the high-quality development and digital transformation of higher vocational education in China, and effectively improve the overall quality of teachers in higher vocational colleges, it is particularly important to construct a set of practical, comprehensive, scientific and reasonable teachers' ability evaluation system.

2 Literature Review

Assessing teachers' ability in higher vocational colleges stands as a core component of vocational education evaluation systems and has long been a focal point in both the theoretical and practical domains of vocational education. Currently, international research primarily concentrates on two key aspects in this area: evaluating the competencies of "dual-qualified" teachers [4] and developing teaching capability evaluation systems [5]. Furthermore, in the era of the digital economy, scholars have begun exploring the utilization of big data to construct models for evaluating teacher teaching ability evaluation model to provide a more comprehensive and systematic assessment of teachers' ability [6, 7]. These studies not only demonstrate methodological innovation but also reflect a focus and consideration towards the development and application within the field of evaluating teachers' ability in higher vocational colleges, as evidenced by their chosen application scenarios.

Research on the evaluation of teachers' ability in higher vocational colleges predominantly focuses on assessing explicit competence qualities in China, such as teaching ability [8–10], innovation capability [11], and information technology application skills [12], while the assessment of implicit competence qualities is relatively scarce [13, 14]. Simultaneously, a plethora of issues persist in the realm of evaluating teachers' ability in vocational colleges in China. These include the lack of vocational education characteristics in the evaluation system, the strong subjectivity of the evaluation subject, the lack of pertinence and discrimination in the evaluation index [15], the formalization of the evaluation process, and the lack of effective correspondence between the evaluation purpose and the evaluation result [16]. These problems have led to the unclear structure of the current research on the evaluation system of teachers' ability in higher vocational colleges, and the existing evaluation system cannot truly and objectively reflect their ability and quality.

In summary, evaluating teachers' ability competence in higher vocational colleges constitutes a complex and systematic endeavor; thus, its evaluation process should embody plurality and diversity. However, most existing studies predominantly focus on external objective factors while offering relatively limited exploration into internal subjective elements such as individual traits among teachers, innovative capacities, and teamwork abilities. Given these considerations, the present study employs the whole process evaluation method of multi-angle and multi-dimension, and constructs the theoretical framework and evaluation index system of the evaluation of teachers' ability in higher vocational colleges based on the CIPP model, which meets the requirements of digital transformation, in order to provide theoretical support for answering questions such as why to evaluate, in what environment to evaluate, and how to evaluate.

3 Research Methods

3.1 The CIPP Model

The CIPP model, proposed by Daniel Stufflebeam in 1967 [17], which comprises four interconnected components: context evaluation, input evaluation, process evaluation, and product evaluation. Each stage is interrelated and closely linked, covering the whole process, each link and key elements of the evaluated object, and has been widely used in education evaluation [18].

3.2 Delphi Method

The Delphi method is a method that involves conducting anonymous consultations and collecting feedback. It is also commonly referred to as the expert consultation method [19]. In this study, we used the Delphi method to screen and determine the evaluation indicators of teachers' ability in higher vocational colleges.

3.2.1 Participants

According to the standard for the number of expert group members stipulated by the Delphi method [2, 20], fifteen experts with rich practical experience and significant academic influence were selected as expert team. The participants included eight front-line teachers who have been engaged in educational and teaching activities in higher vocational colleges (account for 53.33%); four experts are engaged in teacher education research in higher vocational colleges (account for 26.67%); three experts who have been engaged in the assessment, training and supervision of teachers in higher vocational colleges (account for 20%). The basic information of Delphi experts is shown in Table 1.

Table 1. The Basic Information of Delphi Experts

Variable	Indicator	Frequency	Proportion (%)
Age	≥35	1	6.67
	35–40	6	40.00
	41–50	5	33.33
	51–60	3	20.00
Educational Background	Bachelor's degree	1	6.67
	Master's degree	6	40.00
	Doctoral degree	8	53.33
Teaching Experience (year)	≤ 10	7	46.67
	11–15	2	13.33
	16–20	2	13.33
	21–25	1	6.67
	≥ 25	3	20.00
Professional Title	Professor	3	20.00
	Associate Professor	8	53.33
	Other Senior Professors	2	13.33
	Associate Senior Professors	2	13.33

3.2.2 Expert Consultation

In this study, with the help of the electronic questionnaire generated by the "Questionnaire Star" platform and E-mail to solicit expert opinions. The consultation content mainly includes basic information, importance evaluation of all indicators, judgment basis and familiarity.

Likert scale was used to score the importance evaluation, which was divided into five evaluation levels, and the "Revision Opinion" column was set up to extract the opinions on the increase or decrease of index after each level of index. Concurrently, experts are tasked with self-assessing the familiarity and judgment coefficient of the consultation content. According to the results of the initial round of expert consultation, the second round of expert consultation questionnaire is formulated subsequent to the comprehensive index screening criteria and expert revision opinions of the questionnaire preparation group. Following two rounds of consultation and subsequent statistical analysis, the expert opinions will be consolidated to establish the final evaluation index system of teachers' ability in higher vocational colleges. The specific assignment of judgment basis and familiarity is demonstrated in Table 2.

Table 2. The Scoring Criteria of Experts' Judgment Basis and Familiarity

Judgment Basis	The Degree of Influence on Expert Judgment (Ca)			Familiarity (Cs)	Expert Self Assessment
	Large	Middle	Small		
Practical experience	0.5	0.4	0.3	Very Familiar	1.0
Theoretical analysis	0.3	0.2	0.1	Relatively Familiar	0.8
Peer understanding	0.1	0.1	0.1	Generally Familiar	0.6
Intuitive feeling	0.1	0.1	0.1	Not Familiar	0.4
				Not very Familiar	0.2

3.2.3 Criteria for Indicator Screening

According to the numerical screening principles in the Delphi method, we screened and optimized the indicators using the mean (M), standard deviation (SD), and coefficient of variation (CV). The basic judgment criteria were the mean value of the experts' evaluation score (M > 3.5, or 70% of the grade value of the 5-grade scale), the standard deviation of the index score (SD < 1), and the coefficient of variation of the experts' index score (CV < 0.25, or CV = SD/M).

The coefficient of junction was assessed based on the effective recovery rate of the questionnaire, which is generally expected to exceed 70%. The coefficient of reliability (Cr) is determined by the coefficient of sense (Cs) and the coefficient of adjudication (Ca). The calculation formula of Cr is as follows: Cr = (Cs + Ca)/2. In general, when Cr ≥ 0.7, indicating that expert questionnaire consultation result is considered to be highly reliable.

3.3 Analytic Hierarchy Process

The Analytic Hierarchy Process (AHP) is a systematic method for solving complex decision-making problems [21]. In this study, AHP is used to calculate the weight of each evaluation index, which involves comparing the importance of indicators in pairs according to Saaty's relative importance standard [22]. This process establishes a judgment matrix, determines the index weight coefficient, and conducts a consistency test. The formula is as follows:

$$CR = \frac{CI}{RI};\ CI = \frac{\lambda_{max} - n}{n - 1}$$

where CR is the random consistency ratio of the judgment matrix, CI is the consistency index of the judgment matrix, RI is the random consistency index, n is the order of the judgment matrix, λ_{max} is the largest eigenvalue of the judgment matrix. Generally, the smaller the CR value, the more consistent the judgment matrix is. Typically, the CR value is less than 0.1, indicating that the judgment matrix satisfies the consistency test.

3.4 Statistical Analysis

In this study, Excel 2021 was used to input and proofread two rounds of data from expert consultations, and descriptive statistics were calculated for the experts' basic situation and positive degree. IBM SPSS Statistics 26.0 was used to perform statistical analysis and obtain the arithmetic mean, standard deviation, and coefficient of variation of the index scores. Yaahp 12.6 was used to determine the index weight, maximum eigenvalue (λ), and consistency index (CR) through programmed calculations.

4 Theoretical Framework

4.1 The Fitness

The fit between the CIPP model and the evaluation of teachers' ability in higher vocational colleges is primarily evident in three domains. Firstly, given the divergent objectives of talent cultivation in higher vocational colleges, there are discernible discrepancies in the selection of evaluation subjects, the delineation of evaluation contents, the formulation of evaluation standards, the application of evaluation methods, and the purpose and utilization of evaluation. Consequently, the construction and weighting of the evaluation index system should be centered on meeting the needs of talent cultivation and fully reflecting its diversity and complexity. The CIPP model is decision-oriented, taking into account the achievement of talent cultivation goals and the complex changes in teachers' ability and quality, which helps decision makers better understand the current situation of teachers' ability, and then formulate effective improvement measures. Secondly, the process-oriented nature of CIPP enables it to adapt to the stage-by-stage development and advancement needs of the evaluation of teachers' ability in higher vocational colleges. Teachers' ability is defined as a set of unique abilities developed by teachers in the course of their professional development to achieve individual and organizational goals, which integrates teachers' subject knowledge, skills, methods, processes, and affective attitudes and values, and presents clear stage and progression characteristics. This is consistent with the process orientation and formative orientation of the CIPP model. Thirdly, the improvement function of the CIPP model can provide strong support for the optimization, enhancement, and sustainable development of the evaluation system of teachers' ability in higher vocational colleges [23]. The evaluation of teachers' ability is a cyclical and continuous process of diagnosis, improvement, refinement, and optimization. In this process, the CIPP model can provide timely, reliable, and effective information support, thus rendering the evaluation an effective tool to promote work improvement and quality enhancement.

4.2 The Theoretical Framework of Evaluation of Teachers' Ability Based on CIPP Model

Under the background of digital transformation and development, combined with the basic quality and ability of teachers in higher vocational colleges, this study adopts the CIPP model to construct the theoretical framework of teachers' ability evaluation from the aspects of context evaluation, input evaluation, process evaluation, and product evaluation. Among these, context evaluation assesses teachers' fundamental competencies while also considering the new demands and challenges posed by the digital era. Input evaluation examines the adequacy of teachers' resources and preparation, incorporating the allocation of digital resources. In the process evaluation, the application of digital capabilities by teachers in their actual teaching, research, and social service activities should be appropriately assessed. Finally, product evaluation should incorporate an assessment of the tangible outcomes resulting from the use of digital tools and methods.

Specifically, the context evaluation is predicated on the evaluation of the fundamental ability of teachers in higher vocational colleges. It principally conducts diagnostic evaluations of the contents of teacher ethics, professional quality, professional knowledge, educational ability, academic qualifications and degrees, and application ability of digital tools. The input evaluation is predicated on the evaluation of conditional ability of teachers in higher vocational colleges, and principally conducts feasibility evaluation on the contents of teachers' basic teaching level, the level of scientific research, application of digital technology, and industry qualifications. The process evaluation takes the evaluation of teachers' practical ability in higher vocational colleges as the core. It principally conducts formative evaluation on the following: teachers' professional practice, curriculum resources development and construction (e.g. digital textbooks), teaching and research output, participation in social training, technical service training, coaching students to participate in competitions and win prizes, and participation in corporate practice in their professional fields. The product evaluation focuses on assessing teachers' developmental ability in higher vocational colleges. It provides feedback on teachers' ability and improvement suggestions, including a summative evaluation of their teaching innovation, learning and communication, international cooperation, teamwork, and personal development planning abilities (see Fig. 1). In summary, the CIPP model integrates the diagnostic, feasibility, formative, and summative dimensions of evaluating teachers' ability. It illustrates that the evaluation process is a dynamic feedback mechanism, and characterized by continuous diagnosis and improvement. This iterative process of refinement and optimization significantly reflects the dynamic and developmental nature of assessing teachers' ability within these institutions.

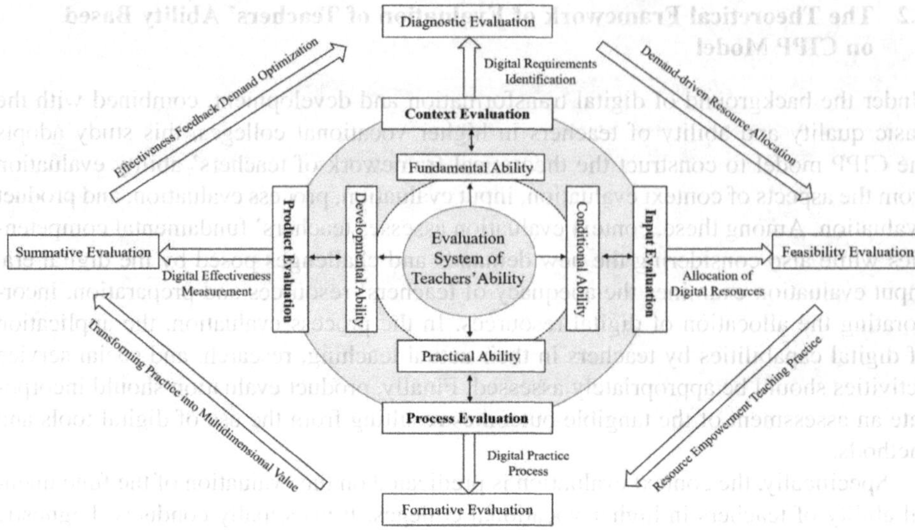

Fig. 1. The theoretical framework of teachers' ability evaluation in higher vocational colleges based on the CIPP model

5 Results

5.1 Construction of Evaluation Index System

Combined the requirements of digital transformation for teachers' ability in higher vocational colleges and review of the extant literature pertaining to the evaluation of teachers' ability [2, 3, 8–16], we have preliminarily constructed an evaluation index system of teachers' ability in higher vocational colleges based on the CIPP model. This evaluation index system consists of four first-level indicators, 20 s-level indicators, and 65 third-level indicators. The Delphi method was subsequently employed to ascertain the set of indicators for evaluating the teachers' ability in higher vocational college.

5.1.1 Coefficient of Reliability

The authority coefficient of experts was statistically analyzed through the distribution of two rounds of expert consultation questionnaires. In the initial round of data collection, fifteen expert consultation questionnaires were disseminated, and fifteen valid questionnaires were retrieved. The coefficient of junction was determined to be 100%. According to the results of the initial round of expert consultation questionnaires, the results showed that Ca was 0.880, Cs was 0.813, and Cr was 0.847. Subsequent to the initial round of expert consultation questionnaires, the second round of questionnaires was disseminated. According to the responses to the second round of questionnaires sent to experts, the results showed that Ca was 0.893, Cs was 0.827, and Cr was 0.860. It can be seen that the value of Ca, Cs, and Cr were all above 0.8 in the two rounds of expert consultation questionnaires, indicating that the expert survey constructed in the evaluation index system of teachers' ability in higher vocational colleges has strong authority and high credibility, meeting the requirements.

5.1.2 Screen and Optimize Evaluation Indicators

According to the results of the first round of expert consultation via questionnaire, the feedback indicated that the first- and second-level evaluation indicators met the retention criteria. Furthermore, the feedback for the majority of third-level indicators also met these criteria, and delete or modify the individual indicators that failed to meet the retention criteria.

Specific suggestions included modifying the secondary indicator "courseware design capability" under professional quality to "application ability of digital tools", as this revision better aligns with the breadth and depth of digital transformation. Additionally, the secondary indicator "1 + X teacher qualification" under industry qualification was proposed to be revised to "vocational skills certificate". This change was suggested to more accurately reflect the nature of the certificate and emphasize an ability-oriented approach. Another modification recommended was changing "public service hours" under social service ability to "social service duration", as this phrasing was considered more precise and standardized. To enhance the evaluation framework's representativeness, operability, and contemporaneity, several indicators were suggested for removal, including "the capacity for course-based ideological and political integration", "classroom organization", "participation in research projects", "micro-lesson competitions", "school-enterprise cooperation", "off-campus laboratory construction", "teaching model reform project research", "publication of innovative educational theory achievements", and "international experience".

In the second round of expert consultation via questionnaire, experts generally endorsed the revised index system. It was confirmed that the first-, second-, and third-level indicators all met the retention criteria. Minor amendments were made to some verbal expressions, while the overall structure and other indicators remained largely unchanged.

5.2 Hierarchical Structure of Evaluation Index System

Following the analysis of two rounds of expert consultation questionnaires, indicators that did not meet the retention criteria were eliminated. Consequently, the evaluation index system for higher vocational college teachers' ability was refined to comprise four first-level indicators, 20 s-level indicators, and 56 third-level indicators (see Table 3).

This system is structured around four primary first-level indicators: Fundamental Ability, Conditional Ability, Practical Ability, and Developmental Ability. Within Fundamental Ability, four second-level indicators are identified: Teacher Ethics, Professional Quality, Professional Knowledge Structure, and Educational Ability. Conditional Ability consists of six second-level indicators: Basic Teaching Ability, Teaching Research Ability, Digital Technology Application Ability, Student Mentoring Ability, Project Research Ability, and Industry Qualifications. Practical Ability is comprised of five second-level indicators: Professional Practical Ability, Curriculum Development and Construction Ability, Ability to Produce Teaching and Research Achievements, Social Service Ability, and Industry Practice Experience. Developmental Ability encompasses five second-level indicators: Teaching Innovation Ability, Learning and Communication Ability, International Cooperation Ability, Teamwork Ability, and Personal Development Planning Ability.

5.3 Determination of the Weights of Evaluation Indicators

The evaluation index system for higher vocational college teachers' ability incorporates multiple indicators with varying attributes and forms. Given that each index plays a distinct role within the overall evaluation, it is essential to clarify their relative importance—specifically, to determine their respective weights [4, 11]. To achieve this, we invited 15 experts to assign weights to each evaluation index based on their individual expertise and understanding. The average of these expert opinions was then used to construct the index judgment matrix, which was subsequently analyzed using the Analytic Hierarchy Process (AHP) to calculate the index weights. The resulting weight distribution for the evaluation indices is presented in Table 3. The consistency of the first-level index judgment matrix was verified through calculation and testing: the Consistency Ratio (CR) was 0.0806, the maximum eigenvalue (λ_{max}) was 4.2153, the Consistency Index (CI) was 0.0718, and the Random Index (RI) was 0.89. Since the CR value (0.0806) is less than the threshold of 0.1, this indicates that the judgment matrix possesses acceptable consistency, thereby validating the reliability of the calculated weight results. Consequently, the construction of the evaluation index system for higher vocational college teachers' ability can be considered complete.

Table 3. The Weight of Teachers' Ability Evaluation Indicators in Higher Vocational Colleges Based on the CIPP Model.

Weight of first-level indicators	Weight of second-level indicators	Weight of third-level indicators
A1 Fundamental Ability (0.3835)	B1 Teacher Ethics (0.3889)	C1 Love the Party and the Country (0.3952)
		C2 Dedication and Moral Cultivation (0.2322)
		C3 Set a Good Example as a Teacher (0.2322)
		C4 Adhere to Academic Ethics (0.1404)
	B2 Professional Quality (0.1881)	C5 Oral Expression (0.4934)
		C6 Written Expression (0.1958)
		C7 Application Ability of Digital Tools (0.3108)
	B3 Professional Knowledge Structure (0.2995)	C8 Teacher Qualification Certificate (0.7500)
		C9 Educational Qualification and Degree (0.2500)

(*continued*)

Table 3. (*continued*)

Weight of first-level indicators	Weight of second-level indicators	Weight of third-level indicators
	B4 Educational Ability (0.1235)	C10 Mental Health Education Ability (0.6667)
		C11 Guide Students to Develop Their Abilities (0.3333)
A2 Conditional Ability (0.3068)	B5 Basic Teaching Ability (0.3374)	C12 Instructional Design Ability (0.1861)
		C13 Teaching Implementation Ability (0.3259)
		C14 Teaching Reflection Ability (0.2463)
		C15 Teaching Evaluation Ability (0.1209)
		C16 Classroom Management Ability (0.1209)
	B6 Teaching Research Ability (0.1610)	C17 Teaching and Research Reform Project (0.4934)
		C18 Published a Teaching Research Paper (0.3108)
		C19 Editor and Co-editor of Textbook (0.1958)
	B7 Digital Technology Application Ability (0.1183)	C20 MOOC Course Construction (0.6667)
		C21 SPOC Course Construction (0.3333)
	B8 Student Mentoring Ability (0.0884)	C22 Guides students in skills competitions (0.4934)
		C23 Guides students on on-the-job internships (0.3108)
		C24 Graduation Project Score (0.1958)
	B9 Project Research Ability (0.2286)	C25 Led a Horizontal Project (0.5000)

(*continued*)

Table 3. (*continued*)

Weight of first-level indicators	Weight of second-level indicators	Weight of third-level indicators
		C26 Presided Over a Vertical Project (0.5000)
	B10 Industry Qualification (0.0663)	C27 Professional Qualification Certificate (0.4934)
		C28 Vocational Skills Certificate (0.1958)
		C29 Social Part-time Job (0.3108)
A3 Practical Ability (0.1752)	B11 Professional Practical Ability (0.0794)	C30 Guide Students to Win Awards (0.3952)
		C31 Number of Horizontal Projects (0.1958)
		C32 Number of Vertical Projects (0.1958)
		C33 Off-campus Training and Technical Guidance (0.2132)
	B12 Curriculum Development and Construction Ability (0.2557)	C34 Number of school-enterprise cooperation courses (0.5396)
		C35 Number of digital textbooks (0.1634)
		C36 Professional Construction (0.2970)
	B13 Ability to Produce Teaching and Research Achievements (0.1332)	C37 Published Academic Papers (0.4934)
		C38 Published Academic Works (0.3108)
		C39 Patent (0.1958)
	B14 Social Service Ability (0.3383)	C40 Social Service Duration (0.2500)
		C41 Social Training Capacity (0.7500)
	B15 Industry Practice Experience (0.1933)	C42 Construction of Off-campus Training Bases (0.7500)

(*continued*)

Table 3. (*continued*)

Weight of first-level indicators	Weight of second-level indicators	Weight of third-level indicators
		C43 Days of Job Rotation Training (0.2500)
A4 Developmental Ability (0.1346)	B16 Teaching Innovation Ability (0.1405)	C44 Demonstration Course (0.5000)
		C45 Famous Teacher (0.5000)
	B17 Learning and Communication Ability (0.1854)	C46 Participation in Domestic Social Training (0.1634)
		C47 Participation in Domestic Technical Services (0.3952)
		C48 Participation in Academic Exchange Activities (0.2781)
		C49 Participation in Practical Exchange Activities (0.1634)
	B18 International Cooperation Ability (0.1065)	C50 International Cooperation Project (0.7500)
		C51 International Curriculum Development (0.2500)
	B19 Teamwork Ability (0.2447)	C52 Participates in Professional (Group) Construction (0.1958)
		C53 Participation in Faculty Team (0.4934)
		C54 Faculty Team Member Evaluations (0.3108)
	B20 Personal Development Planning Ability (0.3229)	C55 Development of Personal Development Plan (0.6667)
		C56 Personal Planning Goal Attainment (0.3333)

6 Conclusion

The evaluation system for higher vocational college teachers' ability is not static; it evolves in response to adjustments in talent training objectives. Therefore, to better adapt to the evolving landscape of higher vocational education reform, the following optimization recommendations are proposed: Firstly, uphold the principle of "classified development and differentiated evaluation". Optimize the governance structure and operation efficiency of higher vocational colleges, and provide basic guarantee for promoting the classified development and individualized assessment of teachers. For example, when constructing an index system that is consistent with the teachers' own development standards, we should take into account the differences between disciplines, combine the actual situation, and set appropriate evaluation indicators; pay attention to the all-round development and personalized needs of teachers, consider teachers' intrinsic subjective factors to stimulate their initiative and creativity. Secondly, deepen the integration of production and education, actively fostering collaborative innovation among schools, governments, and enterprises. It is imperative to proactively establish the necessary conditions and establish the relevant evaluation metrics to motivate teachers to apply their expertise in practical teaching settings. This can be facilitated through corporate internships, on-the-job training, and academic advancement, thereby offering substantial support to teachers to engage in hands-on work within enterprises. Thirdly, ensure teachers are allocated adequate time and resources for professional development. To support academic research and social services, appropriately extend evaluation cycles. Concurrently, proactively explore diverse teacher training models—including school-based training, corporate internships, and domestic and international study visits—to broaden teachers' horizons, enhance their professional competence, and foster innovation capabilities. Finally, strengthen training of teachers' ability to use digital technology. Establish incentive mechanism to encourage teachers to actively participate in digital-based teaching practice, explore the teaching mode of digital intelligence, and incorporate relevant results into the evaluation system of teachers' ability, so as to form a virtuous circle and promote the overall level of teachers.

Admittedly, the proposed evaluation system has been developed through theoretical analysis and subjected to rigorous expert review. Its framework design demonstrates a degree of forward-thinking and holds potential guiding significance. However, it is crucial to acknowledge that the true efficacy of any evaluation system ultimately rests on its practical application outcomes. Currently, this system has yet to undergo extensive empirical validation within the authentic context of higher vocational education. Consequently, the scientific validity of the system's various indicators, the rationality of their assigned weights, and the feasibility of implementation procedures may encounter challenges in real-world operations. Moreover, potential differences in adaptability among educators from diverse disciplinary fields (such as engineering, humanities and social sciences, art and design), along with the tangible impact of evaluation results on teachers' behavioral patterns and institutional management effectiveness, remain to be supported and verified through empirical data. Therefore, to enhance the practical validity and applicability of this indicator system, subsequent research should prioritize conducting pilot tests across multiple disciplines and institutions. Specifically, a phased empirical research plan could be devised: The first phase would concentrate on collecting qualitative data aimed at gaining a deep understanding of teachers' perceptions and feedback regarding various dimensions of the system while identifying potential misunderstandings and operational difficulties for analysis. The second phase will concentrate on integrating both quantitative and qualitative observational analyses, with a primary focus on examining how evaluation results influence teachers' instructional practices and professional development trajectories. Special attention will be given to the practical applicability of indicators related to emerging demands, such as industry-education integration initiatives and innovations in digital teaching. At the same time, flexible adaptation strategies should be formulated in the pilot process, such as adjusting the specific expression or scoring criteria of some indicators according to the characteristics of different disciplines, so as to accumulate experience and provide basis for subsequent large-scale promotion. Through such empirical research, we can accurately assess the system's effectiveness, ensuring it transcends the theoretical level to become a robust tool for advancing the high-quality development of higher vocational education.

In conclusion, constructing a scientific and effective evaluation system for higher vocational college teachers' ability is a long-term and complex endeavor. Its scientific validity and practical effectiveness must be continually tested and refined through ongoing practice.

Acknowledgments. This study was funded by General Research Project of Zhejiang Provincial Department of Education "Construction of Education Quality Evaluation System and Exploration of Innovation Path in Higher Vocational Colleges" (NO.Y202352187), the Key Research Platforms and Projects of Ordinary Higher Education Institutions under the Guangdong Provincial Department of Education "Research on High-Quality Talent Cultivation Models for Cross-Border E-Commerce Programs in Guangdong's Higher Vocational Colleges from the Perspective of Professional Mission" (NO.SK2024C001), and the Teaching and Research Project of Shenzhen Institute of Information Technology "Exploration and Practice of Integrating Ideological and Political Education into Digital Trade Talent Cultivation Models in the Digital Era" (NO.2024kcszzx05).

Disclosure of Interests. The authors have no competing interests to declare that are relevant to the content of this article

References

1. Luo, X., Liu, G.: On Construction of evaluation index system of teachers' ability in higher vocational colleges. J. Hengyang Normal Univ. **43**(5), 129–137 (2022)
2. Lan, J., Xia, J.: The historical retrospection, present situation review and future prospect of vocational college building in China. J. Vocat. Educ. **36**(8), 13–18 (2020)
3. Zhang, W.: Research on the construction of standards and evaluation system for teachers' competences in higher vocational colleges. Continuing Educ. Res. **10**, 69–73 (2023)
4. Li, H., Lin, C.: Research on the ability evaluation of "double-qualified and double-ability" teacher in M university based on fuzzy-AHP. In: Proceedings of the 2019 15th International Conference on Computational Intelligence and Security (CIS), Macao, China, pp. 292–295 2019)

5. Sun, W., Chen, Y., Chen, F.: Research on the evaluation system of vocational college teachers' teaching ability in the digital economy era. In: SHS Web of Conferences (2023)
6. Chen, S., Wang, T., Li, X., Zhu, L., Wu, D.: Research on the improvement of teachers' teaching ability based on machine learning and digital twin technology. J. Intell. Fuzzy Syst. **41**(42021), 7323–7334 (2021)
7. Fu, H., Qi, K.: Evaluation model of teachers' teaching ability based on improved random forest with grey relation projection. Sci. Program., 5793459 (2022)
8. Chen, S.: On the evaluation and development of teaching ability of young teachers in higher vocational colleges——taking Zhejiang Business Technology Institute as an example. J. Zhejiang Bus. Technol. **19**(1), 48–50 (2020)
9. Long, P., Xiang, L., Peng, G.: The construction of evaluation index system of teachers' teaching ability in higher vocational colleges in the new era. Educ. Vocat. **19**, 66–72 (2023)
10. Hu, W.: Initial probe into assessment of teaching ability of teachers. J. China Examinations **10**, 12–17 (2021)
11. Cui, M., Wu, Y.: Evaluation of innovation and entrepreneurship teaching ability of college teachers based on improved BP neural network. J. Jianghan Univ. (Nat. Sci. Ed.) **46**(2), 125–129 (2018)
12. Zhang, Z., Chen, X., Wang, Y.: The Research on Evaluation of Teachers' Informationized Teaching Ability based on TPACK. Mod. Distance Educ. **6**, 66–73 (2017)
13. Zhang, X., Han, C., Dong, Z.: Construction of teachers' ability standard and evaluation system in higher vocational colleges. J. Wuhan Inst. Shipbuilding Technol. **21**(4), 15–19 (2022)
14. Yu, Y., Liu, L.: A review of the research on the ability and quality of higher vocational teachers in China - Based on bibliometrics and CiteSpace analysis. J. Vocat. Educ. **32**, 5–9 (2017)
15. Yin, K.: Research on the professional ability construction of "double-qualified" teachers in higher vocational colleges. Educ. Vocat. **11**, 57–61 (2022)
16. Mo, W., Liu, C., Dai, X.: Teachers' ability evaluation system construction and practice research on the Vocational Colleges. High. Educ. Forum (4), 71–73+77 (2021)
17. Stufflebeam, D.L., Madaus, G.F., Kellaghan, T.: Evaluation Models: Viewpoints on Educational and Human Services Evaluation, 2nd edn., pp. 280–287. Kluwer Academic Publisher, Boston (2000)
18. Zhang, J., Pan, C., Li, H.: Research on construction of quality evaluation index of industry-education integration in vocational colleges based on CIPP model. Chin. Vocat. Tech. Educ. **15**, 54–60 (2023)
19. Naisola-Ruiter, V.: The delphi technique: a tutorial. Res. in Hospitality Manage. **12**(1), 91–97 (2022)
20. Wang, C.: Research on decision-oriented quality evaluation index system of vocational education. Chin. Vocat. Tech. Educ. **27**, 72–75 (2015)
21. Dolan, J.G.: Shared decision-making – transferring research into practice: the Analytic Hierarchy Process (AHP). Patient Educ. Couns. **73**(3), 418–425 (2008)
22. Saaty, T.L.: Fundamentals of the Analytic Hierarchy Process, pp. 15–35. Springer, Netherlands (2001)
23. Cai, R., Zhang, G.: Research on the evaluation of labor education ability in colleges and universities based on CIPP model. China Univ. Teach. **07**, 76–83 (2023)

Data Virtualization for Machine Learning

Saiful Khan[1(✉)], Joyraj Chakraborty[2], Philip Beaucamp[2], Niraj Bhujel[1], and Min Chen[2]

[1] Scientific Computing, Rutherford Appleton Laboratory, Science and Technology Facilities Council, Didcot OX11 0QX, UK
{saiful.khan,niraj.bhujel}@stfc.ac.uk

[2] Department of Engineering Science, University of Oxford, 7 Keble Rd, Oxford OX1 3QG, UK
{joyraj.chakraborty,philip.beaucamp,min.chen}@eng.ox.ac.uk

Abstract. Nowadays, machine learning (ML) teams have multiple concurrent ML workflows for different applications. Each workflow typically involves many experiments, iterations, and collaborative activities, and can take months or even years from initial data wrangling to model deployment. Organizationally, a large amount of intermediate data needs to be stored, processed, and maintained. *Data virtualization* becomes a critical technology in an infrastructure to serve ML workflows. In this paper, we present the design and implementation of a data virtualization service, focusing on its service architecture and service operations. The infrastructure currently supports six ML applications, each with more than one ML workflow. The data virtualization service allows the number of applications and workflows to grow in the coming years.

Keywords: Data Virtualization · Machine Learning · Services · Service Oriented Architecture · SOA · Service Operations

1 Introduction

Developing machine learning (ML) models is a common activity across various disciplines, including the sciences, digital humanities, sports, cybersecurity, business and finance, and engineering. In all ML workflows for scholarly research and applications, numerous experiments often take multiple months, sometimes even a few years to complete. There usually exist different processes for reorganizing the original data in a variety of ways, such as data merging and integration; variable selection; label selection; data reformatting, randomization, and normalization; data partition for training, validation, and testing; and so forth. This list of *data transformation* increases rapidly when one includes other more complicated data wrangling and preparation tasks, such as data cleaning, labeling, augmentation, and feature extraction. A variety of data transformation tasks result in differing datasets for storing more or less the same information. In many ML workflows, these data transformation tasks are performed by individual ML developers, leading to repetitive efforts, ad hoc data management,

M. Luo and L.-J. Zhang (Eds.): SCC 2025, LNCS 16160, pp. 69–84, 2026.
https://doi.org/10.1007/978-3-032-06320-5_6

and unauditable data provenance. It is therefore highly desirable to introduce data virtualization to enhance services to support ML workflows, especially in organizations with multiple ML activities.

Data virtualization is not a new topic, and it has been extensively studied in the field of service computing (e.g., [4,6]). Much of the past research effort has been focused on accessing data remotely and avoiding data duplication. While this remains an essential aspect of data virtualization, the aforementioned requirements from ML workflows suggest a need for data virtualization with smaller-scale virtualization operations at a much higher frequency. In addition, it is highly desirable for such virtualization operations to perform some data processing tasks in addition to data accessing, as otherwise the human effort of processing a series of virtualized datasets remains costly. When an ML development environment is supported by data virtualization, we can anticipate several benefits, including storage savings, data sharing, consistent and repeatable data processing, data provenance, and so on.

In this paper, we present the design and implementation of a data virtualization service for supporting ML developers who work on many ML workflows concurrently. In particular:

a. We propose to extend the concept of data virtualization to address the needs for creating and managing a large number of virtual datasets in ML workflows and to enable virtual datasets to be specified with both path links to proceeding datasets as well as call links to data transformation functions.
b. We designed and implemented a data virtualization service with a service-oriented architecture that features a number of components that were purposely designed for creating, querying, and processing virtual datasets, including a YAML-based specification standard for virtual datasets, a data query engine, and a data processing engine, among others.
c. We explored ML workflows in six applications, confirming the benefits of data virtualization in ML workflows. Meanwhile, these application case studies provided testbeds for the data virtualization service as well as informed many design decisions, e.g., identifying common data transformation functions (i.e., a subset of service operations) to be supported.

2 Related Work

Data virtualization has evolved since the early days of Enterprise Information Integration (EII) systems, which were aimed at providing unified access to heterogeneous data sources without centralizing them in data warehouses. Early EII platforms [6] used mediator-wrapper architectures to map queries over virtual schemas to subqueries executed on the original sources. However, the limited scalability, performance, and source heterogeneity of these systems motivated the development of data federation systems. A comprehensive survey of data federation systems was presented by Gu et al. [4]. The authors found that industrial virtualization requires a significant amount of system infrastructure and concluded that high performance would be contingent upon an advanced architecture [4]. Data federated systems utilize federated queries in various languages (e.g., SQL, SPARQL) and dynamic schema mapping to handle a wide range of data. Gadepally et al. [3] extended this work by integrating multiple data models and engines, including relational, key-value, and array databases.

The virtual knowledge graph [17] introduced flexible graph-based models in place of rigid relational schemas. The research outlined the VKG paradigm and presented evidence that data integration and access can be time-consuming, inflexible, and incur high costs. Furthermore, the authors highlighted that many vendors offered limited scalability, resulting in inefficiencies. Therefore, they advocated for a more comprehensive system integration and identified that system architectures would enable improved deployment [17]. In a survey on performance inference in virtualised systems, Lin et al. [14] demonstrated that inference between virtual machines could adversely impact performance and operational costs. Lans [13] and Muniswamaiah et al. [15] introduced caching, parallel query execution, and hybrid approaches that blended data virtualization with selective materialization to meet performance and scalability demands. Jarwar et al. [9] introduced microservice-based designs to enhance modularity and availability in federated environments. Balakrishnan [1] presented a high-level design that incorporated multiple databases within a single virtualization layer to optimize big data analytics and machine learning; however, there was no report on the implementation of this design.

Kennedy et al. [11] provided evidence for accelerating virtualization to improve performance in cloud computing. Zhang et al. [18] reported the open-source GiantVM – which is a distributed type-II hypervisor for enabling virtualization of a many-to-one combination of resources from various physical machines. Chatziantoniou and Kantere [2] presented DataMingler – a system that facilitates the implementation of data virtual machines, offering schematic flexibility, rapid deployment, and agility in data integration and handling of large datasets. Scheiderer et al. [16] proposed a distributed simulation-as-a-service architecture that supported the training of a reinforcement learning agent using remote simulation, and provided practical evidence that virtualization depended on a facilitating architecture to be scalable. They stated that the current implementation of their architecture could be improved in terms of scalability.

Almost all previous research effort on data virtualization focuses on data access, i.e., accessing explicit data via virtual data. In ML workflows, in addition to data access, there are many data wrangling activities, which are typically unglamorous but costly. In this work, we investigate how data virtualization can address the challenges in ML workflows in general and data wrangling activities in particular.

3 Problem

In many companies or organizations that have substantial machine learning (ML) activities, one major challenge is to provide cost-effective data services to handle a variety of data used and generated in ML workflows. Such data includes not only the source data and model testing results, but also various forms of intermediate data originated from different data transformation processes (e.g., data wrangling, data processing, feature extraction, data partitioning, and others). Examples of some common data transformations are given below:

- **Merge**—Given k datasets of a similar nature from different data sources (e.g., windfarms A, B, C), one needs a merged dataset.
- **Integration**—Given k datasets of different nature from different data sources (e.g., weather data, river data, etc.), one needs an **integrated** dataset.
- **Selection** (Variables)—Given a multivariate dataset with d variables (dimensions), one needs to focus on a subset of variables and thus a simplified dataset with $d' < d$ variables (e.g., selecting the two temperature sensors – among 238 sensors/features – in the Windfarm dataset C.)
- **Selection** (Labels)—Given a dataset with l multivariate data labels, one needs to develop a model for each label, and thus l datasets (e.g., object shape labels for a shape classifier, occlusion labels for occlusion detection, and object size labels for a size classifier, and so on).
- **Normalization**—Given a collection of data objects, some ML training and testing methods can only deal with data objects of a specific format (e.g., images of the same size and aspect ratio, time series data in a pre-defined data range, and so on).
- **Reorganization**—Given a dataset, one needs to reorganize the data in order to use a specific type of machine learning method. For example, a long time series may be reorganized into N data segments; time series prediction models are commonly trained with the former, while time series classification models are commonly trained with the latter.
- **Feature Extraction**—Given a dataset, one needs to transform each data object into its feature representation (e.g., a feature vector for an image, or a feature time series for a raw time series with measured data, and so on).
- **Partition**—Given a dataset with N data objects (labelled or unlabelled), partition it into $a\%$, $b\%$, $c\%$ $(a, b, c > 0;\ a+b+c = 100\%)$ of training, validation, and testing datasets with random object selection. Multiple experiments may involve different specifications of a, b, c and random seeds.

In abstraction, different data transformations can be denoted as different functions $F_k, k = 1, 2, \ldots, N_F$, such that

$$F_k : \mathbf{X}_1 \times \mathbf{X}_2 \times \ldots \times \mathbf{X}_{N_S} \longrightarrow \mathbf{Y}_1 \times \mathbf{Y}_2 \times \ldots \times \mathbf{Y}_{N_D} \tag{1}$$

where, each $\mathbf{X}_i$ is the set of all possible i-th source datasets $(i = 1, 2, \ldots, N_S)$, and each $\mathbf{Y}_i$ is the set of all possible j-th destination datasets $(j = 1, 2, \ldots, N_D)$. Here, the input datasets for and output datasets from each function F_k are ordered, since this is the convention to define most data transformation functions.

In ML workflows, one major shortcoming of the conventional approach is that individual ML developers regularly decide how data transformations are implemented and how the output datasets are stored. Some ML developers effortlessly implement data transformation programs that generate "explicit" output datasets, which occupy a significant amount of space. For example, given large collections of images $\mathbf{X}_{\text{image}}$, ML developers commonly partition them into three datasets $\mathbf{X}_{\text{trn}}, \mathbf{X}_{\text{vld}}, \mathbf{X}_{\text{tst}}$ for training, validation, and testing. If an ML developer wishes to experiment with several partitioning schemes, they sometimes store multiple collections of $\mathbf{X}_{\text{trn}}, \mathbf{X}_{\text{vld}}, \mathbf{X}_{\text{tst}}$ for various partitioning schemes (e.g., different combinations of $(a\%, b\%, c\%)$). Alternatively, and more commonly, one may simply replace old partitioned datasets with new ones in iterative experimentation, resulting in the loss of data provenance.

In some cases, the destination datasets may take more space than the source datasets. For example, when a long time series is transformed into N data segments using a sliding window of length W, the size of the destination dataset (i.e., a collection of time series segments) could be close to W times the original time series (i.e., a long time series). Hence, many ML developers avoid this type of data transformation, although having a collection of N data segments would allow ML developers to utilise more ML techniques.

Although some ML developers write more sophisticated programs to be used in ML workflows by passing path links to training, validation, and testing programs, the lack of a consistent and coherent approach within each workflow and across different workflows undermines quality management in engineering ML models. In Table 1, some major shortcomings of a conventional ML model development environment are shown in the second column (without data virtualization). In the next section, we discuss how data virtualization can address these shortcomings.

4 Approach

In companies or organizations that have substantial ML activities, it is common to have a computational infrastructure to support many concurrent ML workflows. These ML activities are part of the long-term operations within such companies and organizations and involve one or more teams of ML developers and multiple other stakeholders. Hence, a technical solution to address the shortcomings in the middle column of Table 1 is *Data Virtualization.*

Firstly, *data virtualization* does not create explicit copies of the output datasets $\mathbf{Y}_1 \times \mathbf{Y}_1 \times \ldots \times \mathbf{Y}_{N_D}$. Instead, it creates the equivalent virtualized copy for each $\mathbf{Y}_j (j = 1, 2, \ldots, N_D)$, together with the necessary links to the source datasets and the transformation functions. Hence, Eq. 1 is rewritten as:

$$V_k = \mathbf{X}_1 \times \ldots \times \mathbf{X}_{N_S} \longrightarrow [\Phi(F_k), \Psi(\mathbf{X}_1), \ldots, \Psi(\mathbf{X}_{N_S})] \times \mathbf{Z}_1 \times \ldots \times \mathbf{Z}_{N_D} \quad (2)$$

where, V_k is the virtualized version of the original data transformation F_k, $\Phi(F_k)$ is a linking identifier of (or path to) F_k, $\Psi(\mathbf{X})$ is a linking path to a source dataset $\mathbf{X}$, and $\mathbf{Z}_j$ is the virtualized version of $\mathbf{Y}_j$, $(j = 1, 2, \ldots, N_D)$. With $\Phi(F_k)$ and $\Psi(\mathbf{X}_1), \ldots, \Psi(\mathbf{X}_{N_S})$, a virtualization service can dynamically retrieve or compute $\mathbf{Y}_j$ in place of $\mathbf{Z}_j$ $j = 1, 2, \ldots, N_D$ on demand.

In practice, most data virtualization processes are relatively simple, typically $N_S = N_D = 1$, and complex data virtualization can often be decomposed into a

Table 1. Comparison of types of model-development environments: individually-managed data transformations without data virtualization services (middle column) vs. infrastructure with data virtualization services (right column).

Category	Without Data Virtualization	With Data Virtualization
A_1 Version control & reproducibility	Inconsistent data transformation practices, difficulty reproducing experiments due to missing data versions, or transformation details.	Systematic versioning of datasets, transformations, and configurations with easy reproducibility.
A_2 Data operation consistency	Inconsistent data operations (e.g., selection, feature extraction, partition, etc.) lead to issues in the comparability of trained models.	Consistent data operations, potentially through standardized APIs and UIs with validated transformation pipelines.
A_3 Data provenance	Relying on individuals to maintain data provenance, which demands a significant amount of effort, commonly leads to very limited data provenance. Datasets for experiments are often deleted after the experiments are completed.	Automated maintenance of data provenance with complete lineage tracking from source to results.
A_4 Experiment management	Manual experiment tracking, difficulty comparing results across different data preprocessing approaches, and informal parameter management leading to irreproducible results.	Systematic experiment tracking with automated model parameter and metrics logging, comparative analysis tools, and reproducible experiments.
A_5 Integration with ML workflow	Manual integration between data preparation, model training, validation, and deployment phases leads to workflow fragmentation and inefficiencies.	Seamless integration across the entire ML lifecycle with automated pipeline orchestration and standardized interfaces between phases.
B_1 Storage Management	Many ML developers commonly create physical copies of data when only a small portion is needed, or links to source data may not be easy to maintain. This leads to significant space waste.	Infrastructure enables reliable virtualization with logical data access, eliminating unnecessary physical copies.
B_2 Scalability	Limited by individual machine capabilities, manual scaling requires significant developer effort, performance bottlenecks are difficult to identify and resolve.	Automatic scaling across distributed resources, intelligent workload distribution, and performance monitoring with optimization recommendations.
B_3 Data discovery	Over a long period, it is hard to search within the storage space of an ML developer or the shared space of an ML team.	With database and ontological support, easy to query for all virtualized datasets with metadata-driven discovery.
C_1 Effort duplication	Commonly duplicated effort by different ML developers working on similar problems.	Standard queries enable reducing duplicated effort, and with search capability, reduce duplication across teams.
C_2 Model maintenance	Models are maintained by ML developers individually	Models are maintained centrally
C_3 Quality and efficiency	Varying efficiency and varying quality due to diverse programming skills among ML developers.	Efficient (and quality-assured) data operations provided centrally for all ML developers through APIs and UIs.
C_4 Collaboration workflows	Email-based coordination, informal code sharing, difficulty synchronizing work across team members, potential conflicts in concurrent data access.	Structured collaboration with shared workspaces, real-time collaboration features, conflict resolution mechanisms, and coordinated data access patterns.
C_5 Knowledge sharing	Limited or ad hoc sharing among ML developers	Systematic sharing among ML developers as well as teams
D_1 Security and compliance	Inconsistent security practices, difficulty enforcing data access policies, ad hoc compliance with institutional regulations, potential data leakage through uncontrolled copies.	Centralized security policies, role-based access control, automated compliance checking, and audit trails for all data operations.
D_2 Documentation & knowledge management	Scattered documentation, knowledge silos, difficulty transferring expertise when developers leave, inconsistent documentation standards.	Centralized documentation with automated generation from configurations, a searchable knowledge base, and standardized documentation templates.

Note: A: *Core ML Operations*, B: *Resource Management*, C: *Development Efficiency*, and D: *Operational Excellence*.

series of simple data transformations. However, the generalized notation in Eq. 2 can represent some complex data transformations, such as a feature specification based on multivariate data inputs from different data sources.

Figure 1 shows several examples of virtualization operations. The three wind farm datasets consist of wind turbine event records [5]. These datasets are part of the publicly available CARE to Compare collection, which includes 89 years of SCADA time series data from 36 turbines located in three farms in Europe. They were designed to benchmark anomaly detection and fault detection methods in wind turbine operations. In the original offline datasets, each event is stored as a .csv file, with data from different timestamps stored in rows and various features stored in columns. Each of these .csv files has about 50K∼65K rows and up to 957 columns. Because each farm uses a different set of sensors, the datasets have varying numbers of features. Some features are multivariate, resulting in different numbers of columns among the event records.

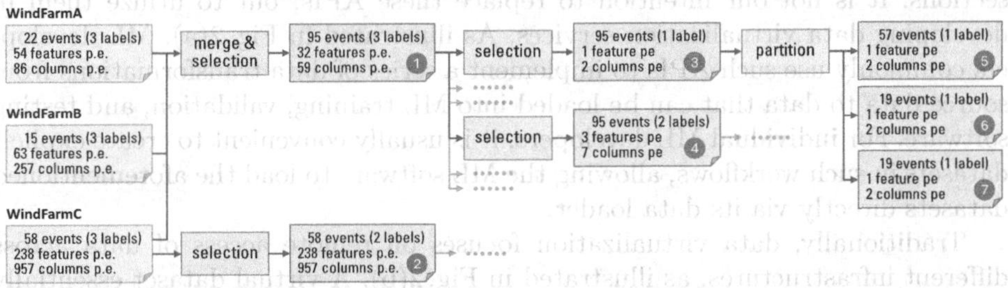

Fig. 1. An example sequence of virtualization operations for transforming three original datasets (on the left) to three virtual datasets for training, validation, and testing (on the right). The figure also shows other possible sequences of transformations, illustrating the need for reducing the storage space while maintaining data provenance.

We can identify 59 columns that are common among the three datasets, select these shared columns, and create a merged dataset as indicated by ❶ in Fig. 1. This virtual dataset consists only of the IDs of 95 virtual data objects and their corresponding link paths to the original event records in the three datasets on the left. The virtual dataset has its own randomized IDs in case of duplicate identifiers among the original datasets.

The Wind Farm datasets were collected for training classification models with one label (*normal* and *anomaly*) and segmentation models with two labels (*event start* and *event end*). Different ML developers may create further virtual datasets, e.g., in the case of ❸, selecting one unary feature to train a classification model, and in the case of ❹, selecting three unary features and one 4-ary feature to train a segmentation model. These virtual datasets can be further partitioned into training, validation, and testing datasets as indicated by ❺, ❻, and ❼.

One can easily notice that there are many options for selecting features in the cases of ❸ and ❹. If one needs to experiment with different feature selections, virtualized datasets can be created with minimal space requirements while maintaining data provenance.

Not only can such data virtualization services improve the cost-effectiveness in data storage, but they can also provide many benefits, e.g., maintaining data provenance, sharing data, sharing data transformation functions, maintaining consistency and comparability among experiments conducted by different ML developers, and so on. In Table 1, we list the benefits of an infrastructure with data virtualization, in contrast to the shortcomings arising from individually managed data transformations without data virtualization services. These shortcomings and benefits are grouped into four categories, i.e., A: *Core ML Operations*, B: *Resource Management*, C: *Development Efficiency*, and D: *Operational Excellence*.

Modern ML and data analysis libraries (e.g., Pandas, Polars, PyTorch, NumPy, scikit-learn, etc.) provide robust APIs to support a wide range of data transformation operations, including the operations mentioned in the previous sections. It is not our intention to replace these APIs, but to utilize them in developing data virtualization services. As illustrated in Fig. 2(a), ML developers commonly use such APIs to implement a series of data transformations from source data to data that can be loaded into ML training, validation, and testing software. For individual ML developers, it is usually convenient to create explicit datasets in such workflows, allowing the ML software to load the aforementioned datasets directly via its data loader.

Traditionally, data virtualization focuses on remote access of data across different infrastructures, as illustrated in Fig. 2(b). A virtual dataset essentially contains only the necessary information to access remote data. Hence, creating a virtual dataset is an action of *specification*, and accessing data is an action of query, followed by the actual data flow to transfer the data to the ML software data loader.

In this work, we extend the notion of data virtualization to include data transformations within an infrastructure. As shown in Fig. 2(c), the notion of specification now includes not only the path links to the proceeding data, which can be explicit or virtual, but also the links for calling data transformation functions. When a data loader in the ML software accesses a virtual dataset, it invokes a series of queries that trace back to one or more explicit datasets, followed by a series of data transformations to load the data into the ML software. Note that ML software may load an entire dataset or individual data objects in a dataset. The specifications, queues, and actual data transformations are all managed by the data virtualization service. Unlike the data flow in Fig. 2(a), the intermediate data is not stored as explicit data files, but as data in the cache to be accessed by the data transformation functions. In the next section, we will detail the design and implementation of the data virtualization service.

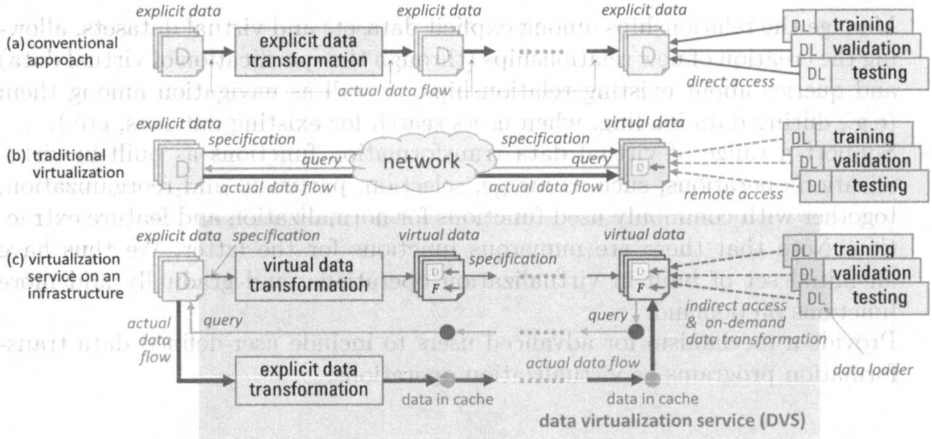

Fig. 2. (a) A conventional data flow for data preparation before training, validation, and testing. (b) A traditional data virtualization workflow focusing on remote access across different infrastructures. (c) A virtualization workflow focusing on data transformations within an infrastructure. While this work focuses on (c), it also supports the hybrid data flows between (a) and (c), and can be extended to include (b). (Color figure online)

5 Design and Implementation

Requirements. A *data virtualization service* is part, or an add-on, of a general-purpose data service. Hence, its capability to support different storage systems (e.g., local server disks, databases, cloud object storage, remote data repositories, etc.), different data types (e.g., audio, videos, geographical data, etc.), file formats (e.g., CSV, NetCDF, PPN, etc.), and different ML libraries (e.g., Pandas, Polars, PyTorch, NumPy, scikit-learn, etc.) depends on the "parent" general-purpose data service. It can interact with other ML development environments (e.g., MLflow, Kubeflow, etc.) for providing data and activating ML jobs. The work reported here focused mainly on the development of a data virtualization service based on the existing capability of the "parent" data service, while we added capabilities to deal with some specific applications on demand.

The design process of our data virtualization service involved two ML researchers who are also co-authors of this paper. The design is specifically tailored to support *ML model development* workflows. Currently, it is not intended for *model deployment*, where dynamic data streams would be encountered. In the context of service development, a data virtualization service should meet the following system requirements:

- Support all storage systems that the "parent" data service can support.
- Support data types and data formats that the "parent" data service can structurally understand (i.e., not stored as opaque data).
- Support all ML APIs available on the infrastructure, where the "parent" data service can access.

- Manage the relationships among explicit datasets and virtual datasets, allowing the creation of new relationships (through the specification of virtual data) and queries about existing relationships, as well as navigation among them (e.g., during data loading, when users search for existing datasets, etc.).
- Support a range of virtual data transformation functions as built-in virtualization operations, such as merge, selection, partition, and reorganization, together with commonly used functions for normalization and feature extraction. Note that there are numerous functions for the latter. We thus have an initial set of built-in virtualization operations, and gradually add more functions on demand.
- Provide a mechanism for advanced users to include user-defined data transformation programs as virtualization operations.

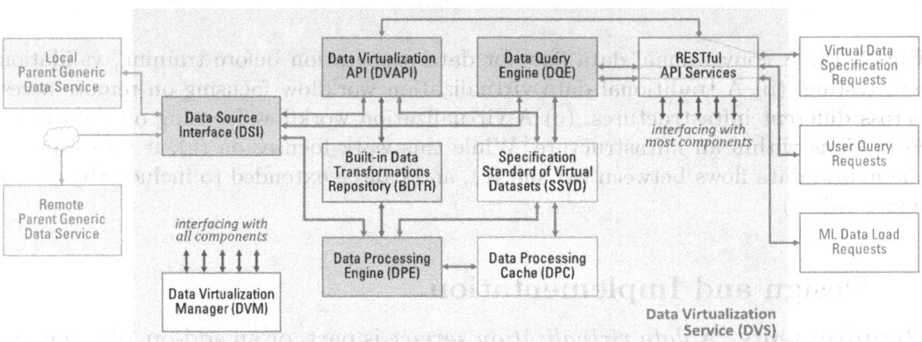

Fig. 3. The service architecture of the data virtualization service and its components.

Design. As shown in Fig. 3, the architecture of the *Data Virtualization Service* (DVS) includes several system components:

- **Data Virtualization Manager** (DVM) – It maintains full knowledge of all current virtual datasets, as well as all explicit datasets managed by the "parent" data service for ML training, validation, and testing. It also enables the creation and removal of virtual datasets. It is the core component of DVS to meet the requirements above.
- **Data Source Interface** (DSI) – This interface allows the DVS to interact with the "parent" data services for accessing explicit datasets managed by the "parent" services. All our current implementations involve only one "parent" data service; we are extending the current DSI to access another "parent" data service, which is located remotely and has a different service architecture.
- **Specification Standard of Virtual Datasets** (SSVD) – It provides a standard file format, e.g., YAML, to specify virtual datasets. It enables a declarative specification of each virtual dataset in a manner that DVM can understand, including details such as metadata, path links to source datasets, data hierarchy, selection criteria, data transformation calls, and randomization settings.

- **Data Virtualization API** (DVAPI) – It provides a programming interface to specify a virtual dataset as well as to query a virtual dataset.
- **Data Query Engine** (DQE) – The query processing unit for processing a query from a data loader or from a user's query, and navigating path links backward (as shown in Fig. 2(a)) or forwards.
- **Built-in Data Transformations Repository** (BDTR) – It provides a list of data transformations, whose unique identifiers can be used by the DVAPI in creating a virtual dataset and by the data processing engine to perform the corresponding data transformations. Some transformations require specialized implementation due to virtualization (e.g., merge, selection, partition, and reorganization), and others are built on top of existing ML APIs (e.g., normalization and feature extraction).
- **Data Processing Engine** (DPE) – The computational unit to invoke data transformation functions during data loading.
- **Data Processing Cache** (DPC) – The DVS maintains a cache space for the DPE to process various data transformations along the dark gray path shown in Fig. 2(c).
- **RESTful API Services** – To maintain the transitions of service states of different activities in DVS (e.g., specifications, queries, data transformation, etc.) [12].

Implementation. We implemented our DVS primarily in Python (version 3.12). The REST API backend was implemented using FastAPI for high-performance, asynchronous request handling, with Pydantic for robust data validation and serialization. Several data transformation functions were built

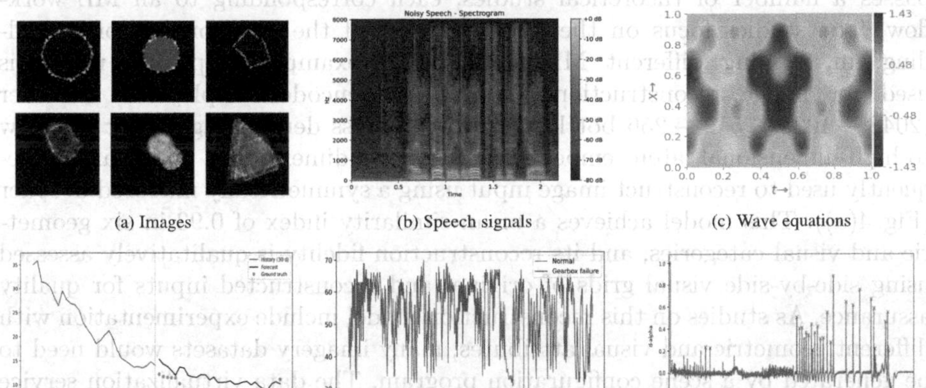

(a) Images (b) Speech signals (c) Wave equations

(d) Time series (water level) (e) Time series (wind turbine sensor) (f) Time series (fusion diagnostics data)

Fig. 4. The data virtualization service currently supports six ML applications. There are multiple ML workflows in each application.

on Pandas and NumPy. We utilized DuckDB for efficient caching and analytical queries with columnar storage and PyArrow for optimized data interchange, along with other Python packages. Although the software for the DVS was developed on a Windows laptop with Linux (WSL) via Docker, it was tested and deployed in a cloud infrastructure in the UK STFC (Science and Technology Facilities Council). The Windows laptop used for the development is equipped with 32 GB RAM and a 14-core Intel i7-13700H processor (20 threads with hyper-threading).

Compared to the conventional approach shown in Fig. 2(a), the overhead of the DVS is unnoticeable primarily on the laptop in terms of speed. The speed difference on the STFC cloud infrastructure is negligible. We anticipate that the speed of users' queries for some virtual datasets will be affected slightly when the total number of virtual datasets increases, while the access queries (e.g., the purple line in Fig. 2(c)) require only a trivial amount of time to track back to the source datasets. Meanwhile, the actual data flow (i.e., the dark gray line in Fig. 2(c)) is faster than the data flow in Fig. 2(a) due to the provision of the data processing cache (DPC). When we consider the time cost for individual ML developers to code and run the data transformation programs as shown in Fig. 2(a), 2(c) represents substantial cost savings.

6 Applications

The data virtualization service described in the previous section has supported several ML workflows. As illustrated in Fig. 4, these applications include:

Embedding in Image Reconstruction and Classification. This encompasses a number of theoretical studies, each corresponding to an ML workflow. The studies focus on the understanding of the functionality of embedding, in training different ML models. For example, a pivotal model is used for image reconstruction. A deep autoencoder employs an encoder (2048 → 1024 → 512 → 256 bottleneck) to compress dense image input into low to high-dimensional latent embeddings (e.g., 256 dimensions), which are subsequently used to reconstruct image input using a symmetrically mirrored decoder (Fig. 4(a)). This model achieves a mean similarity index of 0.93 in six geometric and visual categories, and its reconstruction fidelity is qualitatively assessed using side-by-side visual grids of original and reconstructed inputs for quality assurance. As studies on this reconstruction model include experimentation with different geometric and visual attributes, many imagery datasets would need to be generated by a scene configuration program. The data virtualization service allows ML researchers to create datasets with virtual data objects containing only image attributes. Such virtual datasets can be processed and partitioned in the same way as normal datasets.

In addition to this reconstruction model, there are workflows for training classifiers that use embeddings as an intermediate input. To train a classifier for each geometric category, one needs at least one ML workflow. Because the original imagery data objects are associated with multivariate data labels (e.g., shape, size, color, etc.), the data virtualization service can help select data objects for each sub-label and partition data to ensure the training, validation, and testing datasets with balanced sub-label distribution.

Speech Enhancement. Another application of our data virtualization service is speech enhancement using a UNet-based CNN that takes speech spectrogram images as input and is trained with paired noisy/clean examples to perform denoising (Fig. 4(b)). The encoder consists of multiple convolutional layers that down sample the time frequency map, halving its dimensions at each stage, until a bottleneck of 128 feature channels is reached, using depthwise separable convolutions to limit parameter count. A corresponding up-sampling decoder then reconstructs the denoised spectrogram, which we convert back to a waveform using the inverse Short-time Fourier transform (STFT) (with 50% overlap-add). In standard evaluation sets, this model improves the average PESQ from 1.97 to 2.80, yielding a +12 dB gain in segmental SNR. Due to its small model size and per-frame streaming operation (e.g., 25 ms latency), it can be seamlessly integrated into VoIP systems for robust, real-time audio enhancement.

In addition, there are workflows for studying model pruning. Many interrelated factors, including the input data space, the model task, the network architecture, and the ML hyperparameters influence the effectiveness of pruning. Understanding the impact of these factors requires large-scale, multivariate experiments. For example, the effectiveness of pruning is sensitive to noise and must be evaluated using data with various types and levels of noise augmentation. Since noise augmentation is a form of data transformation, experimentation on different types and levels of noise augmentation can benefit from data virtualization to avoid the storage of many versions of noise-augmented speech data, while maintaining the provenance of the experiments.

River Flow/Water Level Forecasting. One large application of our data virtualization service is the ML development related to river and flood management. In the UK, around 1,500 river gauging stations and 1,000 rainfall monitoring stations measure river flow and rainfall levels. Such historical data is used to develop ML models to forecast volumetric flow rates and water levels at each gauging station. Various ML workflows exist, some for training forecasting models with only station-specific data, some for training models that take the topology of river networks into account, some for training models with both river data and rainfall data, and so on. For example, one workflow utilizes a dual-encoder transformer model that ingests past flow and rainfall records from station S_i ($i = 1, ..., 400$), along with exogenous meteorological inputs, to predict river flow levels for the next 30 days (Fig. 4(d)). This model achieves a mean absolute error (MAE) of 1.28 and a root mean squared error (RMSE) of 1.37.

Data virtualization plays a critical role in supporting the diverse range of ML workflows, as the same data collected by a river gauging station or rainfall gauge is used in many different workflows, often with varying data transformations.

Wind Turbine SCADA Data For Early Fault Detection. Three datasets are collected in different ways. In Fig. 1, we illustrate three types of data transformation, i.e., selection, merge, and partition. Similarly, the application features numerous workflows, which are primarily categorised into two groups. One group includes a large number of workflows for training different sub-models using the time series data of individual sensors. An ensemble model is then derived from the trained sub-models. The ensemble model and the individual sub-models are all classifiers trained using XGBoost. The ensemble models identify impending gearbox faults with 93 % accuracy (F1 = 0.91) across healthy operational states and diverse gearbox failure modes (Fig. 4(e)). The second group includes workflows for training models to detect the starting and ending points of each fault in time series labelled as "anomaly".

Partial Differential Equations (PDE) . There have been growing research activities in developing ML models for approximating numerical PDE solvers. For example, Fig. 4(c) shows the ground truth solution to solve a set of wave equations. Physics-informed machine learning models [10] are trained with spatial or spatiotemporal coordinates randomly sampled from such ground truth data. Physical constraints are incorporated into the loss function used in the training process, steering the learning towards the ground truth solution from scattered data points. However, the effectiveness of training critically depends on the strategies used for data sampling, while the effectiveness of sampling strategies can sometimes be PDE-dependent.

Traditionally, ML developers manually generate, store, and manage thousands of training point configurations, resulting in significant storage overhead and difficulties in reproducing successful experiments. They systematically explore multiple sampling strategies, including uniform grid sampling, adaptive sampling near boundaries, and Latin hypercube sampling for improved space coverage, among others. Furthermore, each strategy requires testing across various point densities (from 1,000 to 100,000 points), different spatial distributions, and multiple random seeds to ensure robustness.

With data virtualization, the sampling strategies are implemented as different data transformation functions to select scattered data points from ground truth data. This enables rapid and reliable data generation in experimental workflows for training ML PDE models, accelerating model development, and maintaining the critical provenance information (e.g., strategy, random seed, etc.) for the repeatability of the experiments.

Fusion Data Analysis. Another application of data virtualization is the analysis of time series diagnostic data from the Mega Ampere Spherical Tokamak (MAST) [7,8] reactor at UKAEA (Fig. 4(d)). The MAST archive comprises experimental discharges "shots" in the order of about 40,000, each capturing high frequency (500Hz) signals with up to 50,000 sampling points per signal. Examples of such signals are deuterium emission D_{alpha}, plasma current (I_p), plasma density $\eta_e(r)$, neutral beam power (P_{NBI}), magnetic field on plasma axis

(B_T), and so on. Making sense of cross-signal relationships is the key to understanding plasma behavior. It enables accurate detection of plasma instability, such as the detection of edge localized modes (ELMs), and thereby facilitates the optimal operation of fusion reactors. To analyze cross-signal relationships, ML developers select multiple signals across shots to identify a subset of relevant signals for each specific task, i.e., confinement mode classification. The data virtualization service allows seamless access to different signals without the need for physical data consolidation, improving the cost-effectiveness of these ML workflows in terms of data storage, programming effort, data provenance, and teamwork.

7 Conclusion

In this paper, we have extended the concept of data virtualization for creating and managing virtual datasets used by many machine learning (ML) workflows. These virtual datasets store not only path links to proceeding datasets, but also call links to data transformation functions. We presented our design of a data virtualization architecture and reported its implementation and six application case studies. While the current data virtualization service is built on top of a local generic data service where explicit datasets are stored, we are developing a service interface with a remote infrastructure that has a different type of generic data service. We also plan to make the software for our data virtualization service available in the public domain as open-source software, and are working on the necessary system documentation.

Our approach offers a cost-effective alternative to the conventional practice, where individual ML developers or teams develop and run their data transformation programs. It enables ML developers to focus on experimental designs rather than data wrangling tasks that support different experiments, and facilitates seamless data provenance management, rather than burdening ML development with rigorous record-keeping. It achieves storage efficiency by replacing explicit datasets with virtual datasets, rather than through the ad hoc removal of used datasets. The six applications currently supported by the data virtualization service demonstrate that with such a service, ML developers are more enthusiastic and more creative in exploring different ML methods and experiments when working on the same datasets.

In addition to the aforementioned interface with a remote infrastructure, we are working on extending the Built-in Data Transformations Repository (BDTR) and introducing version control to ensure the repeatability of ML experiments. We anticipate that the numbers of ML applications, datasets, workflows, and ML developers supported by the data virtualization service will increase gradually in the coming years. This will allow us to measure and analyze the scalability and performance of the service quantitatively as well as assessing the cost-benefit to ML developers and their task performance. Furthermore, we plan to introduce capabilities for visualizing application-specific data provenance, as well as a holistic data ontology, all managed through our data virtualization service.

Acknowledgment. This project was funded by UKRI/EPSRC grant EP/X029557/1.

References

1. Balakrishnan, A.: Data virtualization architecture framework using multi-engine data platforms for big data analytics and machine learning. Int. J. Comput. Trends Technol. **72**(2), 82–91 (2024)
2. Chatziantoniou, D., Kantere, V.: DataMingler: a novel approach to data virtualization. In: Proceedings of the 2021 International Conference on Management of Data, pp. 2681–2685. ACM (2021)
3. Gadepally, V., et al.: BigDAWG version 0.1. In: 2017 IEEE High Performance Extreme Computing Conference (HPEC), pp. 1–7 (2017)
4. Gu, Z., et al.: A systematic overview of data federation systems. Semantic Web **15**(1), 107–165 (2024)
5. Gück, C., Roelofs, C.: Wind Turbine SCADA Data For Early Fault Detection (2024)
6. Halevy, A.Y., et al.: Enterprise information integration: successes, challenges and controversies. In: ACM SIGMOD, pp. 778–787 (2005)
7. Jackson, S., et al.: Fair-mast: a fusion device data management system. SoftwareX **27**, 101869 (2024)
8. Jackson, S., et al.: An open data service for supporting research in machine learning on tokamak data. IEEE Trans. Plasma Sci. 1–10 (2025). https://doi.org/10.1109/TPS.2025.3583419
9. Jarwar, M.A., Ali, S., Chong, I.: Microservices model to enhance the availability of data for buildings energy efficiency management services. Energies **12**(3), 360 (2019)
10. Karniadakis, G.E., Kevrekidis, I.G., Lu, L., Perdikaris, P., Wang, S., Yang, L.: Physics-informed machine learning. Nat. Rev. Phys. **3**(6), 422–440 (2021)
11. Kennedy, J., Sharma, V., Varghese, B., Reaño, C.: Multi-tier GPU virtualization for deep learning in cloud-edge systems. IEEE Trans. Parallel Distrib. Syst. **34**, 2107–2123 (7 2023)
12. Khan, S., Nguyen, P.H., Abdul-Rahman, A., Freeman, E., Turkay, C., Chen, M.: Rapid development of a data visualization service in an emergency response. IEEE Trans. Serv. Comput. **15**(3), 1251–1264 (2022)
13. Lans, R.F.V.D.: Data virtualization in the time of big data. White paper (2022)
14. Lin, W., Xiong, C., Wu, W., Shi, F., Li, K., Xu, M.: Performance interference of virtual machines: a survey. ACM Comput. Surv. **55**, 1–37 (12 2023)
15. Muniswamaiah, M., Agerwala, T., Tappert, C.: Data virtualization for decision making in big data **10**(5), 45–53
16. Scheiderer, C., et al.: Simulation-as-a-service for reinforcement learning applications by example of heavy plate rolling processes. Procedia Manuf. **51**, 897–903 (2020)
17. Xiao, G., Ding, L., Cogrel, B., Calvanese, D.: Virtual knowledge graphs: an overview of systems and use cases. Data Intell. **1**(3), 201–223 (2019)
18. Zhang, J., et al.: GiantVM: a type-II hypervisor implementing many-to-one virtualization. In: Proceedings of the 16th ACM SIGPLAN/SIGOPS International Conference on Virtual Execution Environments, pp. 30–44. ACM (2020)

Integrating RSA-Encrypted NFTs and Blockchain for Medical Data Sharing

L. K. Bang[1(✉)], M. N. Triet[1], H. V. Khanh[1], and N. T. K. Ngan[2]

[1] FPT University, Can Tho city, Vietnam
bangle69.re@gmail.com

[2] FPT Polytechnic, Can Tho city, Vietnam

Abstract. This paper explores the application of blockchain technology in enhancing the management and sharing of medical data. Traditional healthcare data management systems face challenges related to data security, privacy, and interoperability, often resulting in data fragmentation and potential security breaches. Blockchain technology offers a decentralized solution that enhances data security and privacy through immutability and the reduction of centralized risks. Our study evaluates the practicality of an RSA-Encrypted NFT framework for managing healthcare data, demonstrating its consistent performance across various data formats and its integration with the InterPlanetary File System (IPFS) for enhanced data accessibility and durability. Additionally, we conduct a comparative analysis of transaction fees on four EVM-compatible blockchain platforms to assess their economic efficiency and suitability for healthcare applications. Our findings highlight the importance of selecting blockchain solutions that balance cost with functionality to maximize value for healthcare data management.

Keywords: Blockchain · Transparency in Medical Data Sharing · Data Privacy and Security · Smart Contracts · Decentralized Marketplaces · RSA-Encrypted NFTs

1 Introduction

The management and sharing of medical data are pivotal elements in modern healthcare systems. Traditional methods, which frequently depend on centralized databases and manual processes, present significant challenges in terms of data security, privacy, and interoperability. These challenges often lead to data fragmentation, where patient information is dispersed across multiple systems and providers, making it difficult to compile a comprehensive medical history. Additionally, centralized databases are susceptible to hacking and data breaches, potentially exposing sensitive patient information. The lack of interoperability among various healthcare systems due to incompatible formats and standards further impedes smooth data exchange. Moreover, manual processes increase the likelihood of errors in data entry and management [2,15].

M. Luo and L.-J. Zhang (Eds.): SCC 2025, LNCS 16160, pp. 85–98, 2026.
https://doi.org/10.1007/978-3-032-06320-5_7

Blockchain technology has become a viable solution for the challenges faced in data management, providing a decentralized method that boosts security and privacy. The characteristics of blockchain, including immutability and decentralization, are particularly advantageous for handling sensitive data such as medical records. Blockchain's design ensures that data is not centralized, significantly reducing the risks associated with data breaches and unauthorized access. Additionally, the incorporation of smart contracts in blockchain frameworks automates many processes, diminishing the reliance on manual operations and reducing the likelihood of human errors.

Furthermore, our investigation extends to the various applications of blockchain within the healthcare sector, underscoring its capacity to refine both patient care and data management practices. Research conducted by Bang et al. emphasizes how blockchain, when integrated with the Internet of Healthcare Things (IoHT), utilizes smart contracts to improve the privacy and management of patient data [2]. In a similar vein, studies by Son et al. and Le et al. discuss the application of permissioned ledgers such as Hyperledger Fabric, which facilitate fast and secure access to patient data, particularly critical in urgent care scenarios [8,15]. These examples demonstrate the varied ways blockchain technology can mitigate prevalent issues in healthcare informatics.

An assessment of our model, which focuses on RSA key generation, encryption, and decryption processes, confirms its practicality and efficiency for managing and sharing medical data. The analysis shows that our RSA-Encrypted NFT framework operates consistently well across various data formats typical in healthcare records, making it apt for practical use. The demonstrated balance between robust security measures and operational efficiency supports its application in healthcare settings, where protecting sensitive health information is paramount. Furthermore, the integration of decentralized storage solutions, such as the InterPlanetary File System (IPFS), enhances the durability and accessibility of the records, ensuring that medical data remains reliable and accessible across different networks. This methodical approach to managing medical records, prioritizing security and reliability, sets a new standard in medical informatics, advocating for a unified and secure health data management and sharing system.

The evaluation of transaction fees across various blockchain platforms forms a crucial component of our research. Transaction fees significantly influence the operational costs and scalability of blockchain-based solutions. We have conducted a comparative study of transaction fees on four Ethereum Virtual Machine (EVM)-compatible platforms: BNB Chain, Fantom, Polygon, and Celo, with the aim to assess their economic efficiency and suitability for medical data management. Our analysis primarily focuses on three key operations integral to the lifecycle of medical data on the blockchain: transaction creation, NFT minting, and NFT transferring.

Our study underscores the importance of selecting a blockchain platform that optimizes functionality at a reduced cost. The objective is to identify a platform that strikes an effective balance between operational expenditure and system performance, thereby maximizing value for all parties involved in the management and sharing of medical data. The insights derived from our fee analysis assist in determining the overall efficiency and cost-effectiveness of the examined blockchain networks, which aids in choosing the most appropriate platform for setting up robust and transparent systems for medical data management.

In conclusion, our paper delivers a thorough exploration of how blockchain technology can improve the management and sharing of medical data, utilizing encrypted NFTs and IPFS. Through an examination of encryption algorithms and transaction fees, we seek to pinpoint the most suitable blockchain solutions for healthcare contexts. Our research adds to the existing literature on blockchain's application in healthcare by providing actionable insights for developing secure and transparent systems for managing medical data.

2 Related Work

2.1 Blockchain Applications in General Healthcare Systems

The utilization of blockchain technology in healthcare informatics is increasingly recognized for its potential to improve patient-centric systems. Research by Bang et al. discusses how blockchain can be combined with the Internet of Healthcare Things (IoHT), utilizing smart contracts to enhance the privacy and control of patient data [2]. Further investigations by Son et al. and Le et al. focus on the use of permissioned ledgers such as Hyperledger Fabric, which provide rapid and secure patient data access, particularly in urgent care scenarios [8,15].

Duong et al.'s research examines the role of blockchain in creating healthcare systems that are more centered around the patient. Their studies emphasize the significance of data privacy and the empowerment of patients in managing their health records via smart contracts [5,6]. Wilber et al. have also reviewed various blockchain applications within healthcare, noting its extensive potential to support different aspects of the sector, from patient care to pharmaceutical supply chains [17].

In the realm of electronic medical records (EMRs), De et al. and Madine et al. propose blockchain-based models that allow patients to maintain ownership of their data while providing secure access to healthcare providers [9,10]. Innovatively, Shynu et al. have investigated the integration of blockchain with fog computing to improve disease prediction capabilities, which could potentially enhance both data handling and the effectiveness of prognostic medical treatments [14].

2.2 Healthcare and Privacy Protection

Blockchain technology is gaining attention for its potential to enhance the privacy and security of healthcare systems. Shi et al. provided a thorough analysis on the significant impact of blockchain on the security and privacy aspects of electronic health record (EHR) systems [13]. Kumar et al. emphasized the need for healthcare systems based on transparency, not just trust, highlighting blockchain's ability to establish clear, enforceable agreements through smart contracts, despite ongoing challenges [7]. Tith et al. suggested the use of a consortium blockchain to link different EHRs, enhancing privacy while providing secure and transparent access with immutable records [16]. Chen et al. explored how blockchain's intrinsic features such as immutability and decentralization could protect the transmission, storage, and sharing of medical data [3].

Yue et al. developed a blockchain-based framework that enables patients to manage and share their healthcare data securely, employing an access model and schema for organizing personal health information and using Secure Multi-Party Computing (MPC) to maintain privacy during data processing [18]. These instances underscore blockchain's capability to substantially strengthen healthcare data management security and privacy.

Further studies by Zhang, Xue, and Liu have stressed the importance of addressing privacy and security risks in blockchain applications for sharing medical data, recommending the use of sophisticated security techniques such as attribute-based encryption and zero-knowledge proofs [19]. Dagher et al. introduced "Ancile", a privacy-preserving blockchain framework that ensures secure interoperability of electronic health records with stringent access control through smart contracts [4].

Additionally, Vinnarasi A et al. discussed employing permissioned blockchains combined with the Internet of Things to protect healthcare data against unauthorized access while ensuring data integrity [1]. Parmar and Shah reviewed the integration of blockchain and cryptography to improve the security of medical data, aiding adherence to data protection laws [11]. Ponsam, Duvvuri, and Roy outlined a blockchain architecture aimed at the efficient management of electronic health records, focusing on privacy, integrity, and the interoperability among different healthcare entities [12]. Collectively, these research efforts reflect the continuing advancement of blockchain in resolving fundamental challenges in healthcare data management.

3 Approach

3.1 Phase One: Enhancing Transparency in Managing and Sharing Medical Data Utilizing Blockchain and RSA-Encrypted NFTs

Traditional methods of medical data management and Sharing often rely on centralized databases and manual processes, which can lead to several issues. Data fragmentation is a common problem where patient data is scattered across different systems and providers, making it difficult to compile a complete medical history. Security risks are also prevalent as centralized databases are vulnerable to hacking and data breaches, compromising sensitive patient information. Furthermore, the lack of interoperability among different healthcare systems, due to

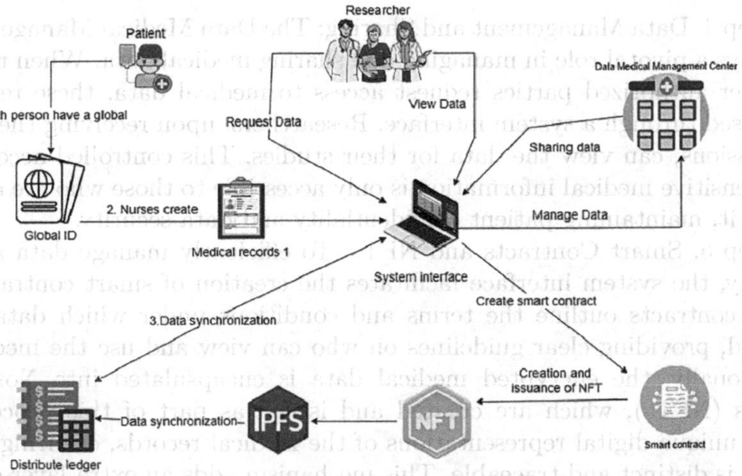

Fig. 1. A structured model for managing and sharing medical data utilizing blockchain.

incompatible formats and standards, hinders seamless data exchange. Additionally, the reliance on manual processes increases the risk of errors in data entry and management.

The Fig. 1 illustrates a structured model for managing and sharing medical data utilizing blockchain and NFT technology, with the added security of RSA encryption. This approach is designed to address several limitations and challenges associated with traditional methods of medical data management and sharing.

Step 1. Assignment of Global ID: The process starts with assigning a Global ID to each patient. This unique identifier is essential for maintaining a consistent and traceable record of the patient's medical history. By having a Global ID, all patient data can be uniformly linked across various healthcare providers and systems, facilitating better coordination and continuity of care.

Step 2. Creation of Medical Records: When a patient visits a healthcare facility, nurses create and update the patient's medical records. These records, labeled as "Medical records 1" in the diagram, include detailed information about the patient's medical history, treatments received, and ongoing care plans. Ensuring the accuracy and completeness of these records is crucial for effective patient management and decision-making.

Step 3. Data Synchronization: Once the medical records are created, a data synchronization process is initiated to securely store and distribute this information using blockchain technology and the InterPlanetary File System (IPFS). Blockchain technology, due to its decentralized nature, helps enhance the security and integrity of the data. By utilizing IPFS, the data is stored in a distributed manner, which reduces the risk of data loss and ensures that it can be accessed from multiple locations when needed.

Step 4. Data Management and Sharing: The Data Medical Management Center plays a pivotal role in managing and sharing medical data. When researchers or other authorized parties request access to medical data, these requests are processed through a system interface. Researchers, upon receiving the necessary permissions, can view the data for their studies. This controlled access ensures that sensitive medical information is only accessible to those who are authorized to use it, maintaining patient confidentiality and data security.

Step 5. Smart Contracts and NFTs: To efficiently manage data access and security, the system interface facilitates the creation of smart contracts. These smart contracts outline the terms and conditions under which data access is granted, providing clear guidelines on who can view and use the medical data. Additionally, the encrypted medical data is encapsulated into Non-Fungible Tokens (NFTs), which are created and issued as part of this process. NFTs act as unique digital representations of the medical records, ensuring that each record is distinct and traceable. This mechanism adds an extra layer of security and helps prevent unauthorized alterations or duplications of the data.

Step 6. Distributed Ledger: The entire process, including the creation and access to smart contracts and NFTs, is recorded on a distributed ledger. This ledger offers a transparent and immutable record of all transactions and access logs. Using a distributed ledger guarantees that there is a permanent and auditable trail of data access and modifications, which is vital for ensuring traceability and accountability in the management of medical data.

Step 7. Enhanced Data Security and Integrity: The synchronization of data between the system and IPFS further supports the secure and distributed storage of medical records. By integrating blockchain and IPFS technologies, the model provides a comprehensive framework for managing and sharing medical data. This framework upholds high standards of security and data integrity, addressing several challenges associated with traditional methods, such as data fragmentation, lack of interoperability, and susceptibility to data breaches. This approach aims to provide a more reliable and secure method for handling medical data, ensuring that it is managed and shared in a controlled and secure environment.

3.2 Phase Two: Integration of RSA-Encrypted NFTs and Smart Contracts for Enhancing Transparency in Managing and Sharing Medical Data System

The Fig. 2 illustrates a model for managing and sharing medical data using blockchain and NFT technology, enhanced by RSA encryption. The process involves several steps, each designed to secure and streamline the handling of medical records.

The process begins at the Data Medical Management Center, which is responsible for the creation and maintenance of medical records. Each patient is assigned a unique Global ID, which is essential for maintaining a consistent and traceable record of their medical history. This unique identifier ensures that

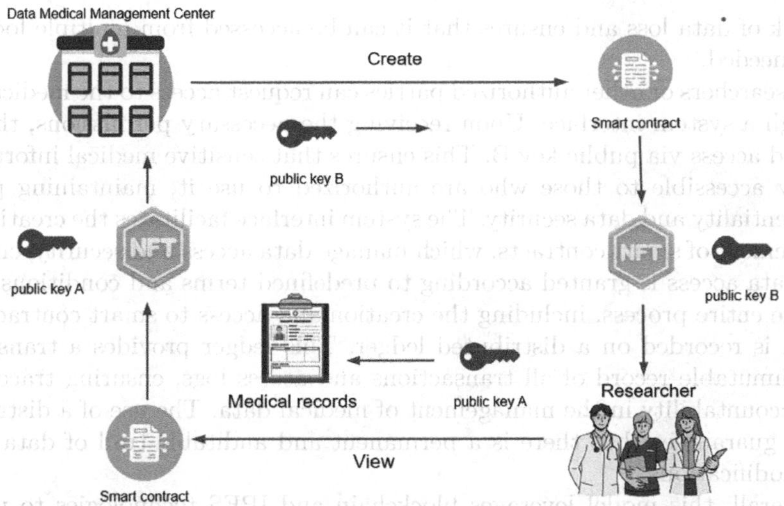

Fig. 2. A model for managing and sharing medical data using blockchain and NFT technology, enhanced by RSA encryption.

all patient data can be uniformly linked across various healthcare providers and systems, facilitating better coordination and continuity of care.

When a patient visits a healthcare facility, the medical staff create and update the patient's medical records. These records, referred to as "Medical Records 1" in the diagram, include detailed information about the patient's medical history, treatments received, and ongoing care plans. Ensuring the accuracy and completeness of these records is crucial for effective patient management and decision-making.

To protect the integrity and confidentiality of the medical data, public key A is assigned for encryption purposes. This encryption ensures that only authorized parties with the corresponding private key can access the information. This step is crucial for safeguarding sensitive patient information against unauthorized access and potential data breaches.

The encrypted medical data is then encapsulated into Non-Fungible Tokens (NFTs). Smart contracts are created to outline the terms and conditions under which data access is granted. These smart contracts provide clear guidelines on who can view and use the medical data, ensuring controlled access and maintaining patient confidentiality. The NFTs serve as unique digital representations of the medical records, ensuring that each record is distinct and traceable.

Following the creation of NFTs, a data synchronization process is initiated. The medical records, now in the form of NFTs, are stored using blockchain technology and the InterPlanetary File System (IPFS). Blockchain technology, due to its decentralized nature, enhances the security and integrity of the data. By utilizing IPFS, the data is stored in a distributed manner, which reduces the risk of data loss and ensures that it can be accessed from multiple locations when needed.

Researchers or other authorized parties can request access to the medical data through a system interface. Upon receiving the necessary permissions, they are granted access via public key B. This ensures that sensitive medical information is only accessible to those who are authorized to use it, maintaining patient confidentiality and data security. The system interface facilitates the creation and enforcement of smart contracts, which manage data access and security, ensuring that data access is granted according to predefined terms and conditions.

The entire process, including the creation and access to smart contracts and NFTs, is recorded on a distributed ledger. This ledger provides a transparent and immutable record of all transactions and access logs, ensuring traceability and accountability in the management of medical data. The use of a distributed ledger guarantees that there is a permanent and auditable trail of data access and modifications.

Overall, this model leverages blockchain and IPFS technologies to provide a structured framework for managing and sharing medical data. This approach aims to address several challenges associated with traditional methods, such as data fragmentation, lack of interoperability, and security vulnerabilities. By integrating these advanced technologies, the model ensures that medical data is managed and shared in a controlled and secure environment, upholding high standards of security and data integrity.

4 Evaluation

4.1 Assessing the Impact of RSA-Encrypted NFTs on Managing and Sharing Medical Data

In examining the application of RSA-encrypted NFTs within the domain of medical data management, a detailed performance analysis was undertaken. The evaluation focused on two primary forms of data that are emblematic of healthcare record-keeping: a digital image, representing typical diagnostic imaging, and a textual data entry, exemplifying routine informational records. This analysis aimed to assess the effectiveness of using RSA-encrypted NFTs in ensuring transparency and security in managing and sharing medical data, evaluating how these technologies can maintain the integrity and accessibility of both visual and textual health records.

The initial phase of the assessment focused on generating RSA keys, a fundamental component of the RSA-encrypted NFT framework. The time required for key generation varied, reflecting the intrinsic fluctuations associated with generating secure cryptographic keys due to the algorithm's reliance on prime number generation. Nonetheless, the recorded times remained within a feasible range for practical application, with an average of about 2645.6 milliseconds.

Subsequently, the process of encrypting and decrypting a 120KB digital image was evaluated. It was noted that encryption processes were generally faster and more consistent compared to decryption, in line with the computational norms of the RSA algorithm where encryption usually requires less computational effort. On average, encryption took about 1135.6 milliseconds, indicating an efficient timeframe that supports timely updates in a patient's health records. Conversely, decryption required more time, averaging 3447.2 milliseconds. This extended duration for decryption is typical with the RSA algorithm, particularly when using larger keys to enhance security, a strategy commonly implemented to protect sensitive medical data (Table 1).

Table 1. Evaluation of Time Efficiency in RSA Key Generation, Encryption, and Decryption for Image

RSA with image(ms)	1	2	3	4	5	6	7	8	9	10
Generating RSA key	2330	2206	2750	2314	2480	2218	2526	3790	2773	2378
Encrypting image	1436	848	913	890	1141	1422	1025	1036	1397	1355
Decrypting image	3234	3946	3337	3796	3379	3360	2449	3174	3830	3267

The evaluation of table data offered further understanding of the framework's effectiveness (referenced as Table 2). The generation of keys showed consistent timeframes, which underscores the reliability of key creation across various types of data. The process for encrypting text data was quick, with an average duration of 1177.1 milliseconds, whereas the time taken for decryption was comparable to that of image data, averaging 3495.1 milliseconds.

These results indicate that the RSA-encrypted NFT framework consistently performs well across diverse forms of data typical in medical records. Although the time required for key generation and decryption is substantial, it remains practical for systems where immediate response is not critical. The swiftness of the encryption process is particularly beneficial in situations where quick updates to medical records are necessary after clinical assessments or treatments.

In the context of managing medical records, the framework needs to strike a balance between stringent security measures and the need for operational efficiency. The data from the evaluation supports the implementation of this framework in medical settings, showing that the time invested in generating RSA keys and decrypting data is justifiable in scenarios that prioritize the protection of sensitive medical information.

Table 2. Evaluation of Time Efficiency in RSA Key Generation, Encryption, and Decryption for Text

RSA with Text(ms)	1	2	3	4	5	6	7	8	9	10
Generating RSA key	2332	2257	2368	2259	2866	2736	2442	1947	2689	2151
Encrypting Text	1496	933	1363	1523	888	781	1483	825	1030	1520
Decrypting Text	3172	3810	3269	3218	4246	3483	4075	3228	3281	3329

Performance metrics indicate that RSA encryption maintains consistent effectiveness across various data types, with key generation and decryption phases proving particularly resource-intensive. This underscores the algorithm's focus on strong security measures. The extended time required for decryption underscores the significant computational effort necessary to access secured data in RSA-encrypted frameworks. Within a medical data management system, achieving the right balance between robust security and processing efficiency is essential. Effective management of this balance ensures that medical data is both protected and processed efficiently. The implementation of RSA encryption in such a system must carefully weigh data security against operational speed to maintain both the integrity and transparency of medical data transactions on a blockchain-enabled platform.

4.2 Testing on the Four EVM-Supported Platforms

The management of medical data using blockchain technology necessitates a careful evaluation of transaction fees, as these fees significantly influence the operational costs and scalability of blockchain solutions. This section presents a comparative analysis of transaction fees across four Ethereum Virtual Machine (EVM)-compatible platforms: BNB Chain, Fantom, Polygon, and Celo. We assess each platform's fee structure to determine its suitability for implementing cost-effective, blockchain-based systems for medical data management, focusing on cost-effectiveness and functionality in various operational contexts.

This study explores how blockchain technology can enhance the management of medical data systems, integrating RSA-encrypted NFTs and IPFS into the system. The analysis highlights three critical functions: data creation, NFT minting, and NFT transfer. These functions are crucial for recording medical information, verifying the authenticity of documents, and securely distributing digital assets among participants.

In evaluating the practicality and performance of these platforms, we focus on the aforementioned four EVM-compatible blockchain platforms: BNB Chain, Fantom, Celo, and Polygon. Each platform is examined for its ability to support key operations necessary for efficient management of medical data. Special attention is given to the efficiency and cost-effectiveness of the transaction processes, aiding in the selection of the most suitable platforms for establishing robust and transparent systems in medical data management.

4.3 Results

The analysis of transaction fees is critical for evaluating blockchain-based systems, particularly within the context of medical data management and sharing. These fees significantly impact the economic viability and sustainability of the system for all users, compensating validators or miners for securing the network and processing transactions.

Our evaluation focuses on three essential operations integral to the functionality of platforms managing and sharing medical data using RSA-encrypted

NFTs: data/transaction creation, minting RSA-encrypted NFTs, and transferring RSA-encrypted NFTs. Each of these functions plays a key role in the life-cycle of medical data on the blockchain:

1. Data or transaction creation involves recording information about medical records on the blockchain. This step ensures that details regarding medical transactions are permanently and transparently stored, which directly influences the cost for users to tokenize their medical data.
2. Minting of RSA-encrypted NFTs transforms medical record details into unique digital assets–RSA-encrypted NFTs–that signify ownership or certification of the data. This process is essential for the digital representation of records, enabling them to be managed more efficiently. Analyzing the fees for minting RSA-encrypted NFTs is crucial to keep the process affordable and accessible for users, thus supporting the operational efficiency of the medical data management and sharing system.
3. The transfer of RSA-encrypted NFTs involves the exchange of ownership of these digital assets between parties. This function is central to the management platform, facilitating the movement and distribution of medical data. The costs associated with RSA-encrypted NFT transfers affect the liquidity and ease of transactions within the system. High transfer fees might limit the frequency of transactions and reduce system utilization, while lower fees could encourage more active management and updating of medical records.

By examining the fees associated with these three functions, we gain insights into the overall efficiency and cost-effectiveness of the blockchain platform for medical data management and sharing. This examination allows us to compare different blockchain networks and select the most suitable platform based on the balance between operational costs and network performance. The goal is to find a blockchain solution that provides necessary functionality at the lowest possible cost, maximizing benefits for all participants in the medical data management ecosystem.

Table 3. Transaction fee

	Transaction Creation	Create NFT	Transfer NFT
BNB	0.0273134 BNB ($16.47)	0.00109162 BNB ($0.66)	0.00057003 BNB ($0.34)
Fantom	0.00957754 FTM ($0.00)	0.000405167 FTM ($0.00)	0.0002380105 FTM ($0.00)
Polygon	0.006840710032835408 MATIC ($0.01)	0.000289405001852192 MATIC ($0.00)	0.000170007501088048 MATIC ($0.00)
Celo	0.007097844 CELO ($0.005)	0.0002840812 CELO ($0.000)	0.0001554878 CELO ($0.000)

Transaction Fee Analysis. Table 3 provides a comparative analysis of transaction fees for three key operations on four Ethereum Virtual Machine (EVM)-compatible blockchain platforms: BNB Chain, Fantom, Polygon, and Celo, with token prices recorded on May 27, 2024. These operations include creating transactions, minting RSA-encrypted NFTs, and transferring RSA-encrypted NFTs, all essential for the management and security of medical data using blockchain technology. By evaluating the fee structures of each platform, we can assess their economic efficiency and suitability for use in systems designed for the transparent management and sharing of medical data through blockchain, RSA-encrypted NFTs, smart contracts, and IPFS.

BNB Chain features a relatively high fee for initiating transactions at 0.0273134 BNB, roughly equivalent to $16.47, which may discourage frequent transactions in high-volume systems. However, the costs for NFT creation and transfer are significantly lower at 0.00109162 BNB ($0.66) and 0.00057003 BNB ($0.34) respectively. This pricing structure suggests that while starting transactions on BNB Chain can be expensive, the subsequent operations involving NFTs–which are key for representing medical data–are considerably more affordable. Thus, BNB Chain may be suitable for environments where initial data entries are sparse, but regular updates and handling of NFTs are more frequent.

Fantom offers a very competitive fee structure that is particularly favorable for systems requiring frequent operations. It charges merely 0.00957754 FTM to create a transaction. For NFT creation and transfer, the fees are reduced to 0.000405167 FTM and 0.0002380105 FTM respectively, making them almost inconsequential. This fee setup positions Fantom as an optimal platform for medical data management systems that necessitate constant updates and rapid transfers of data, as the minimal costs encourage more active and agile data management and sharing.

Polygon also provides very low transaction fees, charging only 0.006840710032835408 MATIC for transaction initiation, approximately $0.01. The fees for NFT creation and transfer are even lower, at 0.000289405001852192 MATIC and 0.000170007501088048 MATIC respectively, supporting cost-effective scalability and regular transaction processing. This fee regime is advantageous for medical data management and sharing systems managing extensive data, enabling cost-effective expansion without sacrificing transaction frequency and data updates.

Celo, aimed at mobile accessibility and cost efficiency, imposes a charge of 0.007097844 CELO (around $0.005) for creating a transaction, with even lower fees for NFT creation and transfer at 0.0002840812 CELO and 0.0001554878 CELO, respectively. This extremely low-cost structure is especially beneficial for stakeholders in economically restricted areas, offering a practical solution for managing and sharing medical data efficiently and affordably. Celo's emphasis on low-cost transactions and a mobile-first strategy can significantly improve accessibility and usability in international markets where cost effectiveness and mobile access are paramount.

By analyzing the transaction fees for key operations across various blockchain platforms, we gain insights into their efficiency and cost-effectiveness in the context of managing and sharing medical data. This thorough analysis of fees helps us systematically evaluate the capabilities and costs of platforms such as BNB Chain, Fantom, Polygon, and Celo. Our objective is to identify a platform that offers an ideal balance between operational costs and system performance, ensuring that the selected blockchain solution provides the required functionality for managing and sharing medical data at the most reasonable cost. This selection process is vital for deploying a system that not only ensures efficient and secure data processing but also maintains low operational costs for all participants, from healthcare providers to patients. This approach is essential for fostering wider adoption and ongoing utilization of the system.

5 Conclusion

The integration of blockchain technology in healthcare data management presents a viable solution to the prevalent issues of data security, privacy, and interoperability. Our research confirms that the RSA-Encrypted NFT framework, supported by decentralized storage through IPFS, effectively addresses these challenges by enhancing data security and ensuring reliable access across networks. The analysis of transaction fees across different blockchain platforms further reveals significant variations in economic efficiency, highlighting the necessity of careful platform selection to optimize operational costs and scalability. Ultimately, our study provides valuable insights into the deployment of blockchain technologies in healthcare, suggesting that a well-chosen blockchain platform can significantly enhance the transparency and security of medical data management systems. This research contributes to the broader understanding of blockchain's potential in healthcare, offering a framework for future implementations that prioritize security, efficiency, and cost-effectiveness.

References

1. A, P.V., Dayana, R., Vadivukkarasi, K.: Healthcare data security using blockchain technology. In: 2023 International Conference on Intelligent Systems for Communication, IoT and Security (ICISCoIS) (2023)
2. Bang, N., et al.: Blockchain-enhanced IoHT: a patient-centric internet of healthcare things platform with smart contract-driven data management. In: International Conference on Advances in Mobile Computing and Multimedia Intelligence, pp. 50–56. Springer (2023)
3. Chen, Z., et al.: A blockchain-based preserving and sharing system for medical data privacy. Futur. Gener. Comput. Syst. **124**, 338–350 (2021)
4. Dagher, G.G., Mohler, J., Milojkovic, M., Marella, P.B.: Ancile: privacy-preserving framework for access control and interoperability of electronic health records using blockchain technology. Sustain. Cities Soc. (2018)
5. Duong-Trung, N., et al.: On components of a patient-centered healthcare system using smart contract. In: Proceedings of the 2020 4th International Conference on Cryptography, Security and Privacy, pp. 31–35 (2020)

6. Duong-Trung, N., et al.: Smart care: integrating blockchain technology into the design of patient-centered healthcare systems. In: Proceedings of the 2020 4th International Conference on Cryptography, Security and Privacy, pp. 105–109 (2020)
7. Kumar, T., Ramani, V., Ahmad, I., Braeken, A., Harjula, E., Ylianttila, M.: Blockchain utilization in healthcare: key requirements and challenges. In: 2018 IEEE 20th International Conference on e-Health Networking, Applications and Services (Healthcom), pp. 1–7. IEEE (2018)
8. Le, H.T., et al.: Patient-chain: patient-centered healthcare system a blockchain-based technology in dealing with emergencies. In: International Conference on Parallel and Distributed Computing: Applications and Technologies, pp. 576–583. Springer (2021)
9. Madine, M.M., et al.: Blockchain for giving patients control over their medical records. IEEE Access **8**, 193102–193115 (2020)
10. de Oliveira, M.T., et al.: Towards a blockchain-based secure electronic medical record for healthcare applications. In: ICC 2019-2019 IEEE International Conference on Communications (ICC), pp. 1–6. IEEE (2019)
11. Parmar, M., Shah, S.: Reinforcing security of medical data using blockchain. In: 2019 International Conference on Intelligent Computing and Control Systems (ICCS) (2019)
12. Ponsam, D.J.G., Duvvuri, S., Roy, S.: Electronic healthcare management system using blockchain technology. In: 2023 International Conference on Circuit Power and Computing Technologies (ICCPCT) (2023)
13. Shi, S., et al.: Applications of blockchain in ensuring the security and privacy of electronic health record systems: a survey. Comput. Secur. **97**, 101966 (2020)
14. Shynu, P., et al.: Blockchain-based secure healthcare application for diabetic-cardio disease prediction in fog computing. IEEE Access **9**, 45706–45720 (2021)
15. Son, H.X., et al.: Toward a blockchain-based technology in dealing with emergencies in patient-centered healthcare systems. In: Mobile, Secure, and Programmable Networking: 6th International Conference, MSPN 2020, Paris, France, October 28–29, 2020, Revised Selected Papers 6, pp. 44–56. Springer (2021)
16. Tith, D., et al.: Application of blockchain to maintaining patient records in electronic health record for enhanced privacy, scalability, and availability. Healthc. Inform. Res. **26**(1), 3–12 (2020)
17. Wilber, K., et al.: A survey on blockchain for healthcare informatics and applications. In: 2020 7th International Conference on Internet of Things: Systems, Management and Security (IOTSMS), pp. 1–9. IEEE (2020)
18. Yue, X., et al.: Healthcare data gateways: found healthcare intelligence on blockchain with novel privacy risk control. J. Med. Syst. **40**(10), 1–8 (2016)
19. Zhang, R., Xue, R., Liu, L.: Security and privacy for healthcare blockchains. IEEE Trans. Serv. Comput. (2021)

Author Index

M. Luo and L.-J. Zhang (Eds.): SCC 2025, LNCS 16160, p. 99, 2026.
https://doi.org/10.1007/978-3-032-06320-5

9783032063199